BE THERE NOW

BE THERE NOW

travel stories from around the world

Julie Rand, Editor
Mike O'Mary, Series Editor

DREAM OF THINGS
DOWNERS GROVE ILLINOIS USA

Be There Now
Editor: Julie Rand
Series Editor: Mike O'Mary

Published by Dream of Things
Downers Grove, Illinois USA
dreamofthings.com

Be there now : travel stories from around the world /
Julie Rand , editor ; Mike O'Mary , series editor.

p. cm.
ISBN 9780988439009

1. Voyages and travels. 2. Travel writing. 3. Travelers' writings. I. Rand, Julie. II. O'Mary, Mike. III. Title.

G465.B4 2012
910/.82 —dc23
2012951075

Dream of Things provides discounts to educators, book clubs, writers groups, and others. Contact customerservice@dreamofthings.com or call 847-321-1390.

First Dream of Things edition

"Demon Blockers" by Jennifer Choban. Previously published by Gear Up & Play (gearupandplay.com), March 9, 2012. Copyright Jennifer Choban 2012. Reprinted by permission of the author.

"Once in a Lifetime" by Terri Elders. Previously published in *A Bird in the Hand: Risk and Flight,* Outrider Press, 2011. Copyright Terri Elders 2011. Reprinted by permission of the author.

"Virtual Travel" by Trendle Ellwood. Previously published in the *Eastern Towne Crier*, Baltimore, Ohio, February 2010. Copyright Trendle Ellwood 2010. Reprinted by permission of the author.

"Still Alive" by Kelly Hayes-Raitt. Previously published in *Gulf Stream Magazine*, Florida International University, Spring 2011. Copyright Kelly Hayes-Raitt 2011. Reprinted by permission of the author.

"Where Light Germinates" by Melissa Heisler. Previously published in *Defining Moments – A Gathering of Women's Journeys*, Amazon Digital Services, 2011. Copyright Melissa Heisler 2011. Reprinted by permission of the author.

"Nowhere" by William Hillyard. Previously published in *Lowestoft Chronicle*, Spring 2012. Copyright William Hillyard 2012. Reprinted by permission of the author.

"Dia de los Meurtos" by Kathe Kokolias. Previously published in *What Time Do the Crocodiles Come Out*, The Troy Book Makers, 2009. Copyright Kathe Kokolias 2009. Reprinted by permission of the author.

"The Happiest Place on Earth" by Dina Kucera. Previously published in *Everything I Never Wanted to Be*, Dream of Things, 2010. Copyright Dina Kucera 2011. Reprinted by permission of the author.

"Perfect Pulpo" by Suzanne LaFetra. Previously published in a different form in *More Sand in My Bra,* Traveler's Tales Guides, 2007. Copyright Suzanne LaFetra 2007. Reprinted by permission of the author.

"In the Footsteps of Fossey" by Irene Morse. Previously published in *Visalia (CA) Lifestyle Magazine*, January 2008. Copyright Irene Morse 2008. Reprinted by permission of the author.

"Open Eye" by Lynn Pinkerton. Previously published by The Shine Journal (theshinejournal.com), October 2011. Copyright Lynn Pinkerton 2011. Reprinted by permission of the author.

"Encounter" by Shannon Huffman Polson. Previously published in *Adventum Magazine*, Winter 2012. Copyright Shannon Huffman Polson 2012. Reprinted by permission of the author.

“Pickles and Hiccups” by Randy Richardson. Previously published by LostintheIvy.com, May 2005, and HumorPress.com December 2006. Copyright Randy Richardson 2005, 2006. Reprinted by permission of the author.

“Turbulence” by Roz Warren. Previously published in a different form by AirplaneReading.org, July 2011. Copyright Roz Warren 2011. Reprinted by permission of the author.

“Horse, Horse, Tiger, Tiger” by Ferida Wolff. Previously published in *Listening Outside, Listening Inside,* Universal Vision, 1999. Copyright Ferida Wolff 1999. Reprinted by permission of the author.

Contents

Foreword

When I was a teenager, we moved from Boston to Chicago. It was summer and it would be weeks before school started. So when my father went off to work, I went out and explored.

I didn't go anywhere in particular on those excursions. I just went. It was a great experience, and now, some 40 years and countless cities, states, and countries later, there is still nothing I enjoy more than coming to a new place and setting out to explore.

I still consider myself a novice by "world traveler" standards, but I've learned a few things along the way. One is that if you pay attention when you travel, you will experience an inner journey that can match or even surpass your geographic journey. Another is that at some point, if you travel enough, you stop saying you are from a specific city or state or country, and you start to think of Earth as your home.

When I put out a call for travel stories for this anthology, I made it clear that I was looking for more than travelogues.

I founded Dream of Things to publish anthologies of creative nonfiction that will fill the gap between popular anthologies that publish stories I regard as "short and sweet," and the *Best American Essays* series, which I love, but which tend to be longer-form. So the goal for Dream of Things anthologies is to be not short and sweet, but short and *deep*.

Be There Now brings together stories from twenty-two contributors set in twenty locations, including Brazil, Bali, Germany, Guatemala, China, Syria, Mexico, France, Nepal, Nicaragua, Peru, Rwanda, Canada, and Costa Rica, plus locations in the United States from Alaska to Disneyland. And in keeping with the goal of Dream of Things to publish stories that have depth, *Be There Now* is travel writing at its most authentic—real people sharing real stories of awe and insight, fear and laughter, humility and humanity as they explore the world around us and seek footholds on their own inner journeys.

I know it is important to "be here now" for family, friends, and career. But I believe it is equally important to take a break from time to time. And so I invite you to take a break today, and allow yourself to "be *there* now" with twenty-two thoughtful people who are willing to take us with them on their journeys around the world and into themselves—journeys that often lead to inspiration, insight, humor, and deeper meaning.

Mike O'Mary, *Series Editor and Founder, Dream of Things*

Introduction

I've been a traveler and I've been a tourist. I never really thought about the difference until I got lost in the backstreets of Suzhou, China. My British friend, Yvonne, and I had decided to go to China at the last minute, so we hadn't made any hotel or train reservations. Somehow we muddled through and managed to find our way from Hong Kong to Beijing, and then on to Suzhou. Even though we were more green than seasoned travelers, this was the first time we'd truly gotten lost.

We wandered the streets for about an hour and eventually made our way back to our hotel. It was only then that I realized that I hadn't really cared that we'd gotten lost, and that in fact it had been exciting, fun and interesting to boot. If we hadn't gotten lost we wouldn't have seen the concrete communal wash houses or gotten glimpses of courtyards filled with hanging laundry and potted plants. We wouldn't have smelled dinner cooking or seen the scrawny dogs lounging in doorways. I realized I had been more curious than afraid, and I knew that whatever happened would be an adventure that couldn't happen at home. It changed my attitude toward travel, and toward life.

The authors of these stories are travelers in the truest sense of the word. They experience the places in which they find themselves and are influenced and changed by those experiences. Not everything goes according to plan, but they adjust accordingly and learn something about themselves in the process.

In "A Quick and Cozy Kidnapping," Ben Bellizzi "adjusts accordingly"—and probably saves his own life (or at least his laptop) in the process. In "Berlin," Jennifer Lang and her mother unexpectedly share views about the Holocaust with a teacher and students in a German school. In "Driving Compassionately," Peter Marmorek learns something about the Balinese approach to life by observing their rules, or lack of rules, of the road. Or consider William Hillyard who, like me, gets lost. His story "Nowhere" about floating on a dark river in the middle of the Amazon jungle will give you chills—partly out of fear, but also because as you read his story, you will tingle with the same curiosity and desire for adventure that got him there in the first place.

People sometimes travel to resolve deep issues: Melissa Heisler visits Peru and works with a shaman to rid her body of its poisons, both physical and spiritual. And Shannon Huffman Polson faces her past when she comes face to face with a grizzly bear in Alaska. But travel can also be as simple as trying new food, as Carol McAdoo Rehme does in "The Jigg's Up," or realizing there's no place like home as does Dina Kucera in her story "The Happiest Place on Earth."

Travel can encompass a once-in-a-lifetime event, like Terry Elders' encounter with a rare scarlet macaw, or Irene Morse's interactions with mountain gorillas in Rwanda. Or "travel" can occur right outside the back door, as Lynn Pinkerton discovers on a visit to artist Georgia O'Keefe's home in Sante Fe, or via "Google Earth," as Trendle Ellwood shows us without ever leaving her house.

"Be there now" can be seen as an injunction, as advice, or as an imperative. The twenty-two stories in *Be There Now* explore just what it's like to truly be there now. We hope you enjoy getting lost in these stories. We know you'll be in good hands.

Julie Rand, *Editor*

Once in a Lifetime

[Guatemala]

Terri Elders

When I first moved to Antigua, Guatemala, my birder knowledge was...for the birds. Or at least my housemate, Kelly, saw it that way

I knew enough about birds to feed spinach greens, not stale muffins, to the domestic ducks at Recreation Park in my hometown of Long Beach, California. Enough to avoid annoying the thirty-pound swans in London's Hyde Park. Enough to understand that silence was golden while trailing knowledgeable birdwatchers in the woods near The House of the Doves at Uxmal. And once, at my grandmother's house in Los Angles when I was ten, I learned the hard way that it's wise to avoid poking a thumb inside a budgie's cage.

But I never quite understood the people, like Kelly, who hiked the John Muir trails with binoculars, packsack and pen.

Or who carried notepads to record every winged creature that soared overhead.

"You lack empathy for everyone who sees the world a little differently from you," Kelly once remarked, when I turned down an invitation to sit on the sundeck and stare into our neighbor's coffee *finca* (plantation). He could sprawl there for hours, tallying the varieties of feathered creatures that fluttered among the overarching trees.

"Birding is the number one sport in America. It even beats basketball," this lifelong Lakers lover announced. "And here there are more than 700 species of birds. You've got to pay attention. This is a once-in-a-lifetime opportunity for a bird watcher!" That afternoon he brought me a guide to local Aves from the bookshop nook facing the Parque Central.

That sunset as we sat on the deck sipping Gallos, the local beer, Kelly cocked his head toward the flame-hued bougainvillea vine draping the brick wall separating our sunken garden from the finca.

"Just listen to that warbler!" he said

I nodded. "I hear it. It sounds like more than one bird."

When it came to bird clatters, I scarcely could distinguish a skylark's carol from a barn owl's screech. Now I heard a harsh, persistent trill, okey dokey, okey dokey, tweet, tweet, tweet, followed by a cacophony of raucous caws and kissy sounds.

Kelly shook his head. "Just one."

"Is it a crow?"

Kelly laughed. "It's a mockingbird! Most likely a bachelor. The males without mates usually are the ones who sing at night."

I took another swallow of my Gallo. "All right, Mr. Ornithology, I'll learn. I promise."

So I studied my manual. I learned that in the highlands (where we were), we had brown-backed solitaires and black-headed siskins, gray silky-flycatchers and blue-throated motmots, white-winged tanagers and green-throated mountain-gems. I loved the rhythm of the names, and hoped soon to be able to single out some of these rainbow-hued creatures.

Gradually I got better at identifying the guests plummeting through our gardens. From time to time I'd point out the iridescent beryline hummingbirds (called "garden jewels" in Guatemala) darting on invisible wings among the fuchsia shrubs, or the turquoise bushy-crested jays nesting in nearby trees.

Sometimes we entertained more exotic visitors—an occasional orange-fronted parakeet or emerald toucanet, attracted to the peachy scent of plumeria in the sunken garden. However, I had yet to see a parrot in the wild.

The manual said that *las guacamayas* (scarlet macaws), the national bird of neighboring Honduras, preferred rainforests, but had been known to frequent higher elevations. These magnificent birds, in population decline throughout Central America because of poachers and deforestation, indeed had been spotted in Antigua, but rarely.

"Most of all, I long to see a scarlet macaw," I confided on New Year's Eve. "That would be a once-in-a-lifetime event, like a total eclipse of the sun."

Kelly eyed me strangely. "Funny you mentioned an eclipse," he said. "In a few months, in July, we're going to have one right here in Antigua, and we can watch it from the sundeck."

In the *Guatemala Times* we read how radio announcers were broadcasting warnings not to look directly at the sun during the upcoming event. When we heard that they advised people to watch the eclipse on television to avoid risk of eye damage, Kelly joked that we could just listen to the eclipse on the radio to ensure complete protection.

We felt lucky. Thousands of people were trekking to Hawaii and Baja to stand in the shadow of the moon. We had merely to pop out to our sundeck to witness darkness at noon. The totality of the eclipse would be nearly seven minutes, the longest for the next 141 years.

Though I wondered how wild birds would react to "the day of two dawns," most of our ex-pat friends predicted that roosters would crow at midday. Local gossip focused on how Maya in the remote rural areas would behave—whether old superstitions would prevail even in 1991. Would pregnant women fear miscarriages? Would shamans predict earthquakes, droughts, or other disasters?

On the day of the eclipse, Kelly and I settled into our deck chairs, with shaded eclipse glasses, macadamias, and mimosas at the ready. By noon dogs began to bay as the moon bit into the western edge of the sun. Birds in the finca drifted upwards to roost in the trees.

Soon tiny spots of light, shining through overhead leaves, showed up on our deck as crescent images. The daylight looked fractured. I glanced at the walls of the Hotel Antigua across the way to see thin wavy lines of alternating light and dark that I later learned were shadow bands, the sunlight distorted by irregularities in the Earth's atmosphere.

Suddenly the sky grew dark. We knew this was second contact and that it was safe to witness the full glory of the sun's corona shimmering overhead. The hibiscus flowers in the sunken garden began to fold inwards. The birds ceased their chirrups. I felt the temperature drop. We watched the stars emerge, and singled out Venus.

Several minutes later we looked away as the sky lightened. Sure enough roosters crowed. Kelly, staring over my shoulder, caught my eye and whispered, "Slowly, slowly turn your head to the right."

I casually swiveled my head until my eyes fell on a scarlet macaw, blending into the magenta bougainvillea bracts. About three feet long, from its crown to the tip of its bright red tail feathers, I figured it for a male.

"Offer it a nut," Kelly prompted. I extracted a macadamia from the dish. The macaw watched me silently. I rolled the nut gently along the brick wall in the bird's direction. He reached out his left talon and snatched it up. In apparent thanks, he emitted a low-pitched throaty squawk, nodded his head, spread his wings and flew back to the finca.

By the time I left Guatemala a year later, I had traded my birder manual for a Spanish textbook, since I was heading to the Dominican Republic to serve as a Peace Corps Volunteer. Kelly, who remained in Antigua, wrote me frequently. No scarlet macaws ever showed up again, he said. Just parakeets and toucanets.

Years later I experienced a second total solar eclipse, this one on the Black Sea. This time I witnessed the confused behavior of terns and other seabirds, but, alas, not a single scarlet macaw appeared.

Not that I was expecting one. I've learned enough about birds, and life, to empathize with those who understand that some things really do happen just once in a lifetime...and are worth waiting for.

Talk About "Embarrasant"

[France]

Dominick Domingo

My three years of private French lessons were taken *after* my stint working for Disney in Paris. In fact, they may have been directly motivated by the horrors of knowing just enough French at the time to be dangerous. Now, I might actually benefit from being submerged in the culture. But at the time, my policy of "One 'Bonjour' goes a long way" was a recipe for disaster.

It's not that I didn't try to prepare. I took the group lessons Chez Disney. But the fact that we were not being graded meant that Marie, our instructor, would go as fast as the weakest link. "Je répète," she would say regularly, all too happy to fulfill our stereotypes with her horn-rimmed glasses and charming lilt. I told myself if she showed up with a white apron and feather-duster I was out of there.

My efforts at learning the language extended to purchasing the entire set of *French in Action* videos. Their title may have had the ring of porn, but they were the furthest thing from it. In fact the series was a total-immersion course broadcast on public television to an episodic soap-opera-esque storyline. But I found the mimes distracting, and the avant-garde, noirish puppets capping each episode brought an unnecessary surrealist tone to the proceedings. I imagine the results would be similar had Fellini produced a *Learn to Speak Italian* series. You'd be lucky to walk away with the ability to say, "Pass the all-seeing eyeballs," or "Please come to the table. The sad clown is served."

To my credit, I am an excellent mimic. Apparently, I had mastered pronunciation, which often left me standing dumbfounded while a native rattled on, having inferred that I was fluent from my impeccable delivery of the phrase "Please direct me to *les toilettes*."

Also to my credit, I was motivated to learn and had little shame about flaunting my horrible French. I banked on the fact that the love-hate relationship the French enjoy with Americans would err on the side of love, and that my limited language skills would come across as charming. Instead, as it turns out, it was assumed I was a local (my perfect pronunciation) who was mildly retarded and favored archaic expressions found only in literature. When attempting to say "I am lost" (something I said often), I would opt for "Je suis égaré" rather than "Je suis perdu." This is the equivalent of saying "I am heavy with child" when you've simply been knocked up.

When it was made clear to me that I spoke the way King Arthur would to his round table, I took to leaving the TV on all night to permeate my subconscious with street French. I had been told this was a very intuitive, direct way to absorb the language. Instead, I would wake exhausted, wondering why the phrase "De quoi parles-tu, Villis?" seemed so familiar. I eventually reconciled it with the more familiar, "Whatchoo talkin' 'bout, Willis?" (It seems even reruns of "Different Strokes" have made it into poorly-dubbed syndication overseas.)

Several incidents in Paris led directly to my enrollment in private lessons upon my return to the States. Some were humorous to me almost immediately, one I gained perspective on over time, and one still comes up in therapy.

The first taught me just how difficult it is to curse effectively or to fling an insult in a second language. While having my backpack checked for stolen goods at the corner grocery store where I had shopped regularly, I rolled my eyes and threw out the stinging reflection, "Welcome to France." Delivered in perfect French, mind you. I could have stopped there. I should have stopped there. Instead, something compelled me to continue on to say, "It wonders not that you all French have won/gained a such grave reputation. You it merit. Shit."

The second incident took place at the neighboring pharmacy, as I had stopped showing my face in the grocery store.

"J'ai besoin de la médicine pour l'estomac," I said with confidence. I held my stomach for emphasis; everyone knows a good gesture can make up for a number of deficiencies in syntax. At this point it is important to understand that I believed myself to have said, very clearly, "I need some stomach medicine." It became immediately clear that this was not the case. The woman began rather frantically flipping through the yellow pages, or *Pages Juenes*.

"Non, non," I protested, "Ce n'est pas un urgence." *It's not an emergency*. I proceeded to describe the desired medication complete with hand gestures. *It's small*. I indicated its size with my hands. *And pink*.

"Tu le bois," I said, miming the international symbol for drinking Schnapps from a bottle. "Comme ça."

"Aaaaaaaah," she smiled, and continued rifling through the book anxiously. I began to suspect she was calling the local Assisted Living facility to see if any retarded adults were missing, when a woman behind me caught wind of our exchange. Everyone in the place had caught wind of our exchange. The place was as windy as a trailer park in Tornado Alley. The woman, who spoke a bit of English, stepped forward.

"Médica*ment*," she said to the woman behind the counter. "Médi*cament* d'estomac."

I had invented the word "Medicine," when in fact the word medicine in French is "Médicament." My Franglish creation "Medicine," (pronounced with a French accent ideally) sounds conspicuously like "Médecin," the French word for Doctor. I had asked repeatedly for a Stomach Doctor. A small, pink Stomach Doctor who drinks.

Another incident was less public but no less humiliating. My Parisian friend Jean-Claude and I were going to Luxembourg Gardens for the day. He spoke not a word of English, and with my horrible French, our communication was limited. It was the perfect relationship.

As we were about to leave my apartment for the metro station, I reached for an umbrella. It looked like it might rain. In other words, we were in Paris in April.

"Non, non," he protested. "S'il ne pleut pas, ça sera embarrassant sur le Métro." Now, here's what I heard: "No, no. If it doesn't rain, it will be embarrassing on the Metro."

This gave me no choice but to launch into a tirade about how the French are too concerned with appearances. Jean-Claude was a banker who lived in Monmartre, and his status-consciousness transcended all language barriers. I was going to get in my two cents worth, about how in the "Land of Opportunity" I wouldn't give a damn how I was perceived, how there is less judgment and more personal freedom, mental and otherwise, how centuries of enduring an oppressive caste system had transmogrified the French psyche into a self-loathing, defeated wasteland of arrogant cynicism which projects its own insecurities about social status onto others.

Now here's what he heard: "Waaaaah-wa-wa-wa-waaaaah." Charlie Brown's parents. The few words he was able to decipher, which by default happened to form the semblance of a complete thought, clued him in to my fatal error. To this day I give him credit for figuring it out, considering that he knew not a word of English. In French, the word "embarrassing" is most often used to mean "cumbersome." What he had suggested to me was simply, "If it doesn't rain, the umbrella will be a hassle to carry on the Metro."

The final miscommunication was not so much comical as, well, tragic. I put it under the category of "missed opportunities," and it haunts me to this day.

When I travel I like to taste the local color, so to speak. Whether with leather-clad young men in Rome with their Caesar-cuts and their scooters, or the more compact, cowl-necked French poets, I feel it my duty to do my part to improve foreign relations. I am a one-man Geneva Convention. The thing I find most intriguing about Frenchmen (all right, European men in general) is that their girlfriends don't have to tell them how to dress. From their strategically unshaven jawlines to their just-random-enough-to-appear-authentic bed head, they have it down. Having grown up with naked soldiers and statues of David on every street corner, idealization of the male form is in their blood, as is the resultant vanity. Their icons include Achilles, Sampson, and Ulysses. In the United States, we have the Marlboro Man, John Wayne, and the Jolly Green Giant.

European men have the right idea. They walk arm in arm, kiss on *both* cheeks. And then there's "Deux du Stade," the yearly calendar issued by the French National Rugby team. Twelve nudies, one for every month, sold for charity. The poses are highly suggestive, vulnerable—*hot.* These guys are not afraid of a few homoerotic undertones. Outside of the odd locker room towel-snap or pat on the ass, it's hard to imagine the NFL following suit.

Simply put, gender roles seem a bit less rigid in France. Sexual orientation a bit more fluid. There is a nearly institutionalized understanding that one or both spouses, well into marriage, will engage in extra-marital activities, often with a member of the same sex. I for one was willing to volunteer for this cultural tradition. Never one to bark up the right tree, I am admittedly one of those homos fixated on the mysterious "bi-curious" subset. So as I looked around the metro at all those well-dressed men with rings on their fingers, I tried to pick out the one ripe for a mid-life crisis.

The downside of more relaxed sexual norms would be what happened to me at BHV. In the heart of the Marais, BHV was perhaps the largest department store I had ever purposefully entered. I'm convinced it had its own zip-code. But I was willing to navigate its daunting network of endless departments in search of art supplies, as inspiration had struck. All my hours at the Louvre had inspired the bright idea to sculpt Jean-Claude on the parquet floors of my apartment. So there I was at ten in the morning deep in the bowels of BHV.

Cortez had an easier time finding El Dorado than I did finding my lump of clay. But my Odyssey was finally nearing its end. I felt it. I saw the signs—*Matériels Artistiques*. The bogus directions, my grave mistake of turning *á gauche* when I should have turned *á droit*, would all be worth it in a few glorious seconds. I could smell the turpentine—I could see the faceless maquettes perched on a high shelf in stiff, unfamiliar poses.

Without warning, a man stepped out into the aisle from behind an end-cap of instructional books. So deliberate was the action that my sneakers screeched as I stopped dead in my tracks. The man was smiling mischievously, like the cat that ate the canary. But this cat had more than a belly full of feathers. It had a record, and possibly bodies in the trunk of its car. Hardest to ignore was what he brandished just beneath the thin layer of denim that seemed to have been stitched around his pelvis. Jeans were worn considerably tighter in Europe, but these Calvins went a step beyond, in a way that said "Eurotrash"...in a way that said "Could this be legal?"

This was the downside to a society with no sexual hangups.This is not to say that the French don't have boundaries.

I had been warned of Parisian etiquette by Jean-Claude. After a roll in the hay, we were exiting my apartment. My shirt was balled up in my hand; I would throw it on while walking.

"You cannot do this," he informed me. "It is not permitted."

What? It is against the law for a man to show nipple on Rue du Turenne? I thought of all the topless women I had seen sunbathing in broad daylight along the Seine during lunch hour. I realized the ordinance was not out of modesty or the brand of puritanical principles we Americans cling to, but out of simple taste. It would be *uncouth* to show nipple on Rue du Turenne.

It was perfectly fine, however, to wag your engorged penis in the company of play-dough, crayons, and faceless mannequins. The closest display of manhood I had seen in public back home was the big, black prostitute on Santa Monica Boulevard who had been warned repeatedly by West Hollywood cops to lose the spandex bike tights. I stepped around the (rather impressive) obstruction and continued toward the more malleable object of my quest. The man followed, his own merchandise inches from my unsuspecting person. I thought it best to completely ignore the distraction, to instead pretend to read labels in French. But it remained there in my periphery, vanishing and then reappearing in a new location in an obscene game of Peek-a-boo, making it unsafe to remove my eyes from the label I was reading. To this day I can tell you, if only in French, the precise chemical makeup of Plastilina Modeling Compound.

At long last, I was rescued.

"Cet homme. Est-ce-qu'il te derange?" *Is this guy bothering you?* The voice was deep and resonant, rattling the foil label I was reading for the fifth time.

"Un peut," I returned, with a half-smile.

The man before me was quintessentially French, possessed of that one kind of rare beauty that comes from a controlled gene pool. I find mixed-race people to be among the most blindingly beautiful, but somehow this formula had its own beauty. The pure Franc and Anglo genes I had seen walking the streets of Paris were unlike any seen in the homogenous, generic amalgam of incestuous inbreeding we call "The Melting Pot." Here were shocking blue eyes bordered by dark lashes a drag queen would kill for, cheekbones that could poke an eye out. Here were dramatic jowls and a strong jaw, marked with dimples to make the Grand Canyon blush. And the lips...those lips so full they don't know the word collagen, and more articulate than their injected American counterparts. American trout pouts are shapeless—about as exciting as a sack of flour. French lips undulate like a roller coaster—keep you guessing.

"Merci," I said, turning my back to the hard-on and facing my new pretend-boyfriend. The man was up for the charade, and he proceeded to plant a familiar kiss on both of my cheeks. We closed the gap between us yet more, to crowd out the offending penis, the one that had molested my perfectly innocent quest for art supplies. Apparently feeling shunned, it eventually wandered on its way.

We made a bit of small talk, Jean-Luc and I. Most men in Paris were named Jean-something-or-other. Yes, I lived in the area. Yes, I was visiting from the United States, and no, I did not have plans later in the day. He lived in the area as well. And as it turns out, so did his fiancée. He was to be married the following day. He told me this as if it were necessary information, his voice lowering to a whisper and eyes scanning the room.

"C'est vrai?" I delivered this with a sigh, but secretly looked forward to fulfilling my bi-curious fantasy.

"T'es mignon," I flattered. I welcomed any opportunity to practice my French. And flirting in French was like extra credit.

"Toi aussi," he smiled. When the smile relaxed there was an insistence in his eyes—an urgency I cannot describe. I would try to draw him from memory later, erasing and re-drawing due to the elusive nature of both memory and fantasy. It was everything I could do not to reach up and feel the stubble of his military cut beneath my fingers, to grab the sandpapery base of his skull and pull those lips to mine, right there among the *Matériels Artistiques.* I guess relaxed mores are contagious.

I could tell he wanted it as much as I did, but he had greater reason to resist. His eyes scanned the room one more time, and then he leaned in and whispered into my ear, "Is it possible that you can meet me later this afternoon? We can go to your apartment."

Hell yeah, I thought.

"Bien sur. À quelle heure?" *At what time?*

"À treize heures. Dehors." *Three o'clock. Outside.* He nodded toward Rue Rivoli.

Now, the root of the misunderstanding…the ever-so-minute gap in comprehension that would make us nothing more than two ships passing in the night…that would reduce him to a haunting visage impossible to capture in charcoal…was this: Trois heures is very different than treize heures. I have never been very good with numbers, even in English. And I'm even worse with military time, which is the norm in France. Treize heures, or thirteenth hour, is one in the afternoon. Trois heures, which is what I heard but *not* what was said, indicates three in the afternoon. So as I stood on the sidewalk in front of BHV at three in the afternoon, realizing my error, I began to wonder what lucky pedestrian had wandered by at one o'clock. I hoped whoever it was, he sent Jean-Luc off into married life with a smile.

Día de los Muertos

[Mexico]

Kathe Kokolias

A young Purépechan woman lingers on the sidewalk watching the procession of cars. A black woven shawl draped around her shoulders, she holds a bundle of long-stemmed orange marigolds in both arms and waits patiently to cross the cobblestone street. The narrow passageways of Patzcuaro are clogged with traffic, carloads of foreign tourists and Mexicans pouring into town for *Día de los Muertos* (Day of the Dead).

I am visiting this gracious colonial city high in the Sierra Madre del Sur in the state of Michoacan to witness the festivities that I've heard about for many years. While the holiday is observed all over Mexico, the city of Patzcuaro and the nearby island of Janitzio draw thousands of visitors each year from around the country and the world.

Día de los Muertos is rooted in the ancient Aztec belief that death is not the end of life but a passage to another realm where the souls of the dead exist. It spans two days and was originally observed in mid-summer. After the Spanish Conquest, Roman Catholic priests changed the dates of Dia de los Muertos to November 1 and 2, to coincide with the observance of All Saints Day and All Souls Day as part of their plan to convert the indigenous people.

To welcome the souls who will journey from the Otherworld back to this one, people visit cemeteries and decorate graves with flowers, candles and candy in the shape of skulls and skeletons, *calaveras.* It reminds me of the Memorial Days of my childhood in upstate New York when my family drove across town to the Elmwood Hill Cemetery to tend my grandparents' graves—only without the candy skulls.

Finally there is a break, and the woman winds her way through the stopped vehicles honking their horns. She floats between bumpers, oblivious to the racket and the stench of exhaust. I follow in her path, toward the display booths lining the *zocalo* (main town square). A week ago, vendors erected rows of plywood stands on the perimeter of the zocalo that are now teeming with golden marigolds, the traditional flower of the dead, as well as yellow mums and gladioli in lavender, pink, and white. Flowers by the truckload are sold as quickly as they're delivered. Tables are crammed with basketfuls of *pan de muertos* (bread of the dead), small round loaves imprinted with crosses and skull designs, that will be offered to the dead or enjoyed by the living. Miniature skeleton sculptures are decorated with icing to adorn graves or to keep as souvenirs. I buy two sugar skeletons and ask the vendor, "Por favor, where I can get the bus to the lake?" He gives me my change and points to a corner on the other side of the square.

The packed bus lurches along the shore of Lake Patzcuaro towards the outskirts of Tzintzuntzan, a village whose name in Purépecha translates to "land of the hummingbird." Parked cars line the shoulder of the narrow highway that divides the town cemetery into two sections. I enter the main section through a great *arco* (archway), filled with thousands of marigolds. Children play tag among the headstones while their families clean weeds from around the graves, which they then decorate with flowers and votive candles. One little boy holds a miniature toy coffin and laughs when he pulls its string and a skeleton pops up.

I recognize the Purépechan woman from the zocalo. Her shawl folded on the ground beside her, she sits next to a grave with three other women, talking and laughing as they divide bundles of blossoms into smaller bouquets. They seem oblivious to the tourists around them snapping photos and shooting videos. Families of the departed have placed bottles of Coca Cola and tequila, and baskets of pan de muertos on the mounds of earth as if preparing a table for dinner. Sugar skulls balance on the headstones. By nightfall a banquet of rice, beans, enchiladas, tamales, tacos, and fruit will be set out—all the sustenance souls might need to recuperate from their long journey.

Deep blue plastic tarps, the color of the Virgin of Guadalupe's mantel, cover the chilly ground next to the graves for those who will keep the all-night vigil singing, reminiscing, and communicating with the dead through prayer. They will be on the lookout for signs that the souls are with them, such as a strange shadow, a whisper, a bottle tipping over for no reason, or the feeling of being touched when no one is close by.

Back in Patzcuaro a few hours later, I watch an explosion of red, green, and white fireworks splinter the shrouded night sky. November 1 is *La Noche de los Angelitos* (the Night of the Children), and the fireworks serve to open the heavens and guide the souls of the little angels back down to earth. Young boys dart through the crowded street, their faces covered with macabre paper masks or white paint. They carry carved pumpkins with a candle lit inside and extend an opened hand to tourists. I assume they are trick-or-treating like kids on Halloween in the United States and rush to a nearby store to buy a bag of candy. But when I offer them a treat they look puzzled. Finally I understand what they are trying to tell me. They don't want candy. They are collecting money to help their families pay for this holiday—the cost of food and drink for the dead and for the hoards of out-of-town relatives. They murmur "gracias" as I give them each a few pesos.

On my way to a restaurant, I run into an artist whom I met on my last trip to Patzcuaro. She invites me to a ceremony later that evening in her home, and although I had planned to spend the night in the cemetery on Janitzio along with hundreds of others, I gratefully accept her invitation. Waiting until after dinner to buy flowers, I find that the plaza, a sea of activity for days, is now empty except for a lone vendor standing over two bedraggled bunches of mums. "Dos pesos" (about thirty cents), he says. I snatch up the flowers and hurry to catch a ride to the village of Erongaricuaro.

Around midnight, a dozen women and men gather in a cozy adobe house. They work in silence preparing for the ceremony, building an *ofrenda* (altar), in the center of the living room. They light tall, white candles and thick sticks of copal incense, and sprinkle orange flower petals in the shape of a cross on the smooth stone floor. The mums I brought are arranged in a terracotta vase alongside the altar. A thick, worn black ledger passes around the circle from hand to hand as each person writes down the names of loved ones who have died, names that will be read out loud during the ritual. Entering the names of the beloved people in my life who have passed away, I realize that I've given them only an occasional thought over the years, usually on their birthday or the anniversary of their death.

During the ceremony, a blending of Aztec and Catholic traditions, I understand few of the words that are partly spoken, partly sung in Spanish and in an ancient indigenous tongue. But when the long list of names is read just before dawn, I recognize those of my family and friends—Mom and Dad, Yiayia and Papou, Stefan, and Pete—being honored in prayer in this little house high in the mountains of Mexico. At that moment I am no longer a casual observer of a sacred tradition, but a part of Día de los Muertos.

The next year, I stop off at Patzcuaro on my way south to the Pacific Coast. Día de los Muertos is a few days away, and my friend, Jane, is building an altar to her fiancé who died unexpectedly the previous fall, a month before their wedding. Benjamin's photograph is in the center of the altar, surrounded by candles, loaves of pan de muertos, a bottle of tequila, a pack of Marlboros, and his frayed cowboy hat.

Chicken wire molded into the shape of a cross will be filled in with flowers and placed on the altar. Picking up a marigold and trimming off the excess stem, Jane begins a story, "I remember the time..." and tells how she and Benjamin met and how they built this lovely home on a hillside overlooking Lake Zirahuén. Entwining the flowers one-by-one into the wire mesh, we share stories, laugh, and cry, and soon the cross is bulging with blossoms. We center it on the altar, scatter the remaining petals on the altar cloth, and step back to admire our work. Jane lights the candles and pours two glasses of their favorite Mexican white wine, and then we raise our glasses to Benjamin's smiling face and drink a toast in his honor.

Demon Blockers
[China]

Jennifer Choban

Driving from Panjin to Dan Dong should only have taken three or four hours, but the bus was taking the scenic route and the first snowstorm of the year had hit that November morning. So instead, it took nine hours. Nine hours, one pit stop. And I was in that special monthly state of "enjoying being a girl."

Ally, my travel partner, had been in China for several years, and was accustomed to how bad the bathrooms can be. When the bus stopped at a small cement building in the middle of nowhere she said, "It's going to be ugly," and headed for the bathroom stalls.

"Stall" is really too generous a word for the structures I'm talking about. There are no doors and the walls are only waist high. Actually, bathroom is too generous of a word. It was a trench to squat over. Everyone uses one trench. You can imagine how pretty this gets. But I am not one to stand on ceremony. When you gotta go, you gotta go. I had to go and take care of the other issue as well.

I followed my friend into the bathroom. There were three stalls. I was fourth. "Well, I'm not going to stand and stare at her while she pees," I thought and backed out of the bathroom. I was new to China. Chinese women walked past me and did stand, staring at the people peeing. You do what you have to do. So I went in, stared, and then finally took my turn to squat with a middle-aged, nondescript Chinese woman staring at me.

Now, in recognition of the fact that half the people in the world never have to deal with this, let me just state the obvious and say that inserting a tampon is a very private thing. It's not just that I had never before done it in front of a stranger. I had never done it in front of anyone at all. Not in front of my former husband with whom I had lived for thirteen years, nor in front of my mother, who when I first came of age, described what to do, told me a funny story about her first time, and then left me to it. Nope. The Chinese woman was my first. Northeastern China is one of many corners of the world where women don't use tampons. I can't imagine what the woman thought. Quite possibly it was as disturbing for her as it was for me.

Back on the bus, I reflected on my new experience and was drawn back to a conversation I'd had with Zou Jun, the Chinese matriarch of the family I lived with, a few weeks before. I had seen people making small fires and putting some kind of special paper into them. Zou Jun told me the fires were to honor one's deceased relatives and that prayers go up on the smoke. The papers I had seen were money, going to relatives in heaven who needed the money there. (The fact that heaven had an economy and that one could be broke there was vaguely disturbing to me, but I often find descriptions of heaven disturbing.) She went on to say that if you burn money for someone, you must not wear skirts or dresses when it warms up in the spring. The spirits want to come back and can fly up into you that way.

Suddenly I sat upright in my seat on the bus and called to Ally who was stretched out in the seat across from me. We were in a remote area of China and yelled back and forth in English without worrying that someone else would understand.

"Hey, Ally," I said, "you know how Zou Jun said that if you burn money for your relatives you're not supposed to wear skirts because a spirit will fly up your twat? Well, do you think you're safe if you have a tampon in?"

She howled with laughter. "Maybe if it's a super!"

Then she went on about the lost marketing opportunity. "Oh, my God, China is the biggest market in the world. Tampax is going about it all wrong. They should be selling them as demon blockers."

Demon blockers indeed. That's what we called them for the rest of the trip, and that's probably what we'll call them for the rest of our lives.

Still Alive

[Syria]

Kelly Hayes-Raitt

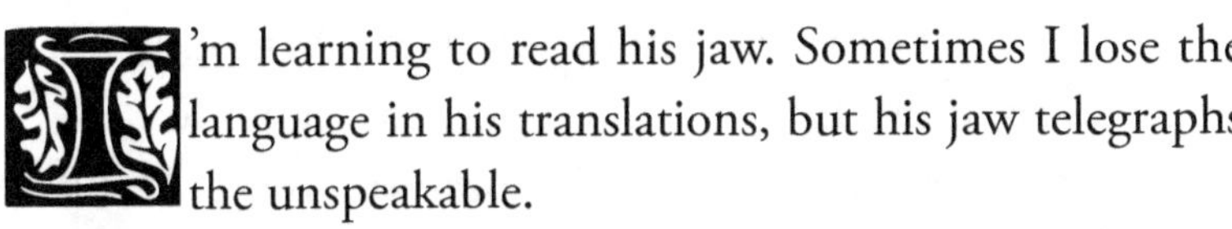

I'm learning to read his jaw. Sometimes I lose the language in his translations, but his jaw telegraphs the unspeakable.

But tonight, I can't see it. We're facing each other, squaring off in the shadows over outdoor vanilla sundaes laced with crisp kiwis and strawberries, arguing about whether I should accompany him to pick up his food rations from the United Nations. The UN had suspended food giveaways, but now he finally has an appointment to pick up four months of food for his family.

"This could cause you problems," I lean forward, dropping my voice, glancing sideways at the oblivious diners. I want to go, but not at his expense. He wants me to go, to document the lives of Iraqi refugees who fled to Syria following the U.S. invasion and after the ensuing violence that drove him and another two million Iraqis from their homeland. "But your file could get marked because you are with an American," I warn.

I'm on precarious ground, too. Volunteering in Damascus for the summer with a delegation to assist refugees and to gather research for a book, I worry about jeopardizing both the local church that is sponsoring me and the refugees who share their stories for publication. "Your file could get marked," I say again.

When I first met Abdullah, five years ago in Iraq just weeks before the war, he was talkative, chatting up American human rights activists at our budget hotel in Baghdad as he served us breakfasts of olives and boiled eggs. Olive-skinned and slender like the other waiters, he stood out with his English and his trusting way of ingratiating himself with us Americans. He brought us farewell gifts as he made sure to collect our contact information, and he wrote group e-mails every few months, filling us in on post-invasion life.

During my final hours in pre-war Iraq, Abdullah brought me flowers, tenderly grown in the garden at the Palestine Hotel across the street, where he moonlighted as the gardener. I carried those dusty marigolds all the way to the Iraqi-Jordanian border before scattering them. I wasn't sure how much of Iraq I wanted to carry home.

But I returned to Baghdad a few months later, and Abdullah and I shared tea on the dreary second floor of that Palestine Hotel, dark then due to another electrical blackout. Over hot, sticky chai, Abdullah confessed his marriage was failing and professed his admiration for me. It was a tender, desperate moment.

I pretended I didn't understand.

The last time I saw him, he was protesting in the street, joining a workers' demonstration for a salary increase from the Palestine Hotel, an act that would not have been allowed under Saddam Hussein.

His e-mails were newsy and sometimes impatient at my predictable questions about security, electricity, and "re-building," to which his answers remained predictably the same—except for the e-mail he sent after he voted. His optimism bubbled from my computer screen amidst his familiar fragments and comical misspellings. Then came the e-mail about the Palestine Hotel coming under fire and his final effort to rebuild the garden he had so faithfully tended. It's no longer alive.

His emails became more angry and urgent. Next he wrote of his aborted effort to resettle in Amman, Jordan, a trip taken the day before his forty-third birthday. After a long and expensive bus ride, border guards refused to allow this fleeing Baghdadi into Amman because he was carrying too much luggage, which included his treasured English dictionaries.

Knowing it was too dangerous to return to Baghdad, he persisted, hiring a driver to taxi him to Damascus, arriving just months before I did in May 2008.

During the March 2003 invasion, his family had holed up at the Palestine Hotel along with international journalists covering the war. This was the hotel where two German photojournalists were shot and killed while documenting the American tanks grinding into Baghdad. U.S. soldiers, mistaking the photographers for snipers—or targeting them as journalists—aimed at the seventh floor balcony of the

Palestine Hotel, and fired. As a hotel employee, Abdullah helped remove the bodies.

He tells me this story five years later in Damascus, where he has been joined by his estranged wife, two daughters, ailing father, and a sister. I schedule Abdullah to address our delegation, and I watch his face unwind as he holds us spellbound with his uncensored recounting of the early days of the U.S.-led invasion. He wants us to understand the enormity and the specificity of the war's impact. His smile is loose and full, and his chiseled face relaxes with each person he engages.

Abdullah is magnetic in his unwavering quest for peace. His serenity draws out his audience and he answers every question sincerely, forthrightly. I'm mesmerized by his ability to control his expressions and voice, although I can see there's a lot coiled in his wiry body.

Handsome in a navy blue suit, crisp shirt, and royal blue tie (his uniform as a waiter at a fancy restaurant), he tells of asking Marines why they were coming into his country. "We are coming to put in democracy and freedom," he recalls their answers. "At the time, I thought it might be [possible]. Where is that promise now?"

When asked if he thinks about returning to his homeland, Abdullah's jaw tightens: "No, I don't think about going back to Iraq."

I had forgotten how proud he is. His e-mails during the last five years, with their mangled English, were somewhat obsequious. But he appeared at my hotel my first night in Syria looking dapper in a freshly pressed shirt and dark green slacks, short hair slicked to perfection. I was an unkempt mess in travel-weary slacks, a bulgy shirt meant to hide my feminine form, and hair pulled back from my sticky face. We went for coffee in the Old City, and he answered my questions about his life as a refugee, spilling information I had not heard before.

Assisting American journalists had cost him dearly in Iraq and could cost him here in Syria, too. In Baghdad, his name had been put on a "list," and his family's house had been stormed by soldiers while his young daughters cowered upstairs. "Iraqi soldiers, not U.S soldiers," he clarified. "But same hammer."

Weeks later, my ice cream softening in the Syrian heat while we debate about the UN food giveaway, I remind him, "Your file could get marked because you are with an American." He leans back and aims his piercing eyes into mine. "I am a free man."

We agree to an overly elaborate plan. Although it's open to the public, I'm not sure I'm allowed to visit the UN food distribution site, and I'm not sure if my presence will jeopardize my Syrian sponsor. Suspicions fly about the government monitoring our e-mails, about eavesdropping secret police, about the identity of a forceful stranger who boards our group's tour bus in southern Syria and demands we drive him home. I'm not sure any of these suspicions are true, or not true, and I'm not sure why I feel such uncertainty. I do not feel like a free woman.

To be among the 200 people who will receive the UN rations, Abdullah decides to arrive before 7:00 am—two hours early—to get his assigned number. Once he has his number, according to our plan, he will call me with an estimate on the length of his wait if he feels it's safe.

I get his whispered call. He's number 118. Refugees had started arriving as early as 6:00. He tells me to join him.

The cab drops me at a gate wallpapered with lists of names. People mill about while waiting for their turn to sit in a stifling tent in order to wait to stand in a meandering line to enter a trailer to get a card that allows them to stand in another line to wait to finally gather their staples and board a truck that will take them home.

Abdullah nervously greets me in front and tugs me through the crowd to regain his place in the last of the lines. I stand behind him, using his wiry body to shield me from the UN worker's sight. He graciously maneuvers me into the iota of shade created by a small overhang from the tent.

A Middle Easterner wearing a baby blue UN bib approaches authoritatively and questions Abdullah in Arabic.

"What?" I lean in as the man walks away.

"He wanted to know who you were, and I told him you were with me," he says defiantly, his taut jaw barely moving.

I am overwhelmed by the lines. Lines into a trailer. Lines into another tent. Lines of people who used to create the lines of Iraqi society: teachers, engineers, architects. Educated, middle-class professionals now reduced to standing in the blistering sun for free flour and olive oil and dishwashing detergent.

It's a slow, quiet process. Each person hands over paperwork. A clerk at a folding table radios some unseen bureaucrat and bangs an approving stamp on the flimsy paper. Three men methodically haul six bags of rice and two dozen boxes of staples onto the backs of small flatbed trucks that will transport the refugees and their food home. Little is said.

Abdullah later tells me that he avoids other refugees. "They discuss subjects I don't want to talk about," he says vaguely. "Some of them are violent." He heard about a refugee in Damascus who ran into the Iraqi who had killed his brother back in Baghdad. The refugee and his cousin tracked down the killer in his new Syrian neighborhood and beat him to death. "I'm a stranger in this country, and I just want to live in peace."

Just before it is his turn to enter the long tent and hand over his paperwork for approval, Abdullah whispers through gritted teeth for me to wait for him by the gate. I wander over to the trailer to see if I can find someone in charge to talk with me.

A UN volunteer, a young Danish man in his twenties, is suspicious of me. "I was wandering by and saw the UN logo and wanted to see what you are doing," I gush. "It's great work." He tells me to contact the main office.

He elbows me through the gate, as I wonder why there's not a sense of accomplishment, of wanting the world to know about the UN's heroic attempts to help the 1.2 million Iraqi refugees who have flooded Syria during the last five years. I've been to the "main office" and met with the same level of secrecy and suspicion. There's not even a PR pamphlet available at the UN's front desk. Later, I will meet individual UN staff, and they will gladly share their knowledge and openly convey what the UN is doing. But today, amidst the refugees with uncertain futures and uncertain pasts, even the UN rep feels insecure.

Outside the food distribution center gates, Abdullah motions for the truck driver to pull over and pick me up from the side of the road. I try to initiate small talk with the driver through Abdullah's translating, but my companion's clamped jaw tells me there is more to this scenario than I understand.

The driver is a private driver, a taxi driver of sorts, who is making good money hauling refugees and their rations. He might do six runs today. Abdullah later tells me he thought the driver worked for the Syrian government and he over tipped him. I think it's a good thing that UN money is trickling into unemployed Syrians' hands, too, but Abdullah is jittery, watching the rearview mirror, and doesn't relax until he has stopped en route and put me into a cab back to my hotel. Suspicion is everywhere.

Over the summer, Abdullah and I become a team of sorts, with him suggesting ideas for me to write about and translating my interviews. He schedules a "day in the life" for me to see refugee life firsthand by accompanying him to a pharmacy, to a medical clinic with his father, to his home for lunch, and to the UN with his daughters to pick up school supplies and uniforms.

He sets up an interview for me with a pharmacist who had been providing free prescriptions to refugees in exchange for reimbursement from the UN. In May, the Syrian pharmacist and his wife had refused to fill Abdullah's father's prescription, telling him they didn't have the medication, and that he should come back tomorrow. "Coming back" for Abdullah's elderly, sight-impaired father involved an expensive roundtrip of catching first a minibus and then a cab. After his dad returned to the pharmacy and was turned away twice more, Abdullah went in and learned that the pharmacist was no longer honoring refugee prescription receipts because his pharmacy hadn't been reimbursed by the UN.

I ask around and learn that non-profit activists had "heard stories" that pharmacists were denying Iraqis prescription drugs but they hadn't gotten any documentation. Abdullah somehow convinced the pharmacist to talk with me, to allow me to take his photo and post it on my blog. It was a tough interview, partially because Abdullah's English isn't strong enough to carry nuanced translating, and partially because the pharmacist went through several paragraphs of social niceties before telling his story.

For six weeks earlier this summer, Tony Ankire and his wife, Rima Toume, weren't reimbursed by the UN for drugs they dispensed free to Iraqis. They typically gave a month's supply of prescriptions to an average of 150 patients each day, running up a deficit they claimed was 2.3 million Syrian pounds, or about $46,000 U.S. They punch out the number twice for me on their calculator so there's no misunderstanding.

While Abdullah and I drink the proffered thick Arabic coffee from demitasse cups over the glass top pharmacy counter, Ankire and his wife describe a second reason they no longer serve Iraqis: "Some of them shout and make problems," Ankire says. "We lost old customers when the Iraqis came in."

"Because of Iraqis' psychological issues," Abdullah translates, without looking at me. I study his proud profile, his immobile jaw. It hurts to see his smile tighten and his gaze drop as he translates something so humiliating.

I later ask him how it felt to listen to Iraqis being insulted. He tells me he had told the pharmacist to feel free to say whatever he wanted. I know Abdullah gracefully argued with him, based on the length of their untranslated conversations and on the set of that eloquent jaw.

Abdullah says he explained to the pharmacist that many Iraqis have had brothers killed, daughters kidnapped. Indeed he is right. Every Iraqi I meet has had a relative, a friend, or a neighbor who was killed or kidnapped. *Every* Iraqi. No one speaks of the details when they all share the same unspeakable burden. So they mark their days, niceties spilling through tight polite smiles, eyes lowered to avoid recognizing reflected tragedy.

Until an outsider shows up.

On the steps leading into one of the two medical clinics for refugees, I am immediately surrounded by injured Iraqis baring their unhealed wounds and pressing their maimed children into my arms. The Syrian-Arab Red Crescent provides Iraqi refugees with a wide spectrum of healthcare, but the cash-strapped refugees themselves must meet a twenty percent co-payment, an amount that is beyond their reach, especially for those requiring ongoing treatment.

I tour myriad waiting rooms. This clinic is another exercise in patience for the 300 to 400 people who wait for hours each day to be seen by a doctor. Cramped rooms crowd pushy women and crying babies. Corridors overflow with listless men, too tired or injured or scared or hopeless to complain. There isn't enough health care in the world to heal these thousands, tens of thousands, of aching people.

Abdullah's father has been here since 8:45 this morning. He waits five hours. Recuperating from eye surgery, he can barely afford the co-payment and the cab fares to pick up his eye drops.

To avoid gossip among the prying eyes of his Syrian neighbors, Abdullah's dad has told them I'm a UN worker visiting the apartment he shares with his son and a daughter. To further avoid suspicion, he's invited Abdullah's daughters, Amina and Lolou, to join us for lunch.

Lolou, thirteen, greets me with an exuberant announcement, translated by her father, that she's decided she wants to adopt my cat whose photos she's seen on my computer. Over roasted chicken and mint salad shared family/picnic-style on a cloth on the floor, fifteen-year-old Amina declares she wants to be an engineer, tossing her lively turquoise-scarved head assertively.

Abdullah's home, like other refugees' homes I've visited, is spotless. It is a typical two-bedroom flat with virtually no furniture. Before leaving Baghdad two years ago, Abdullah's father gave away all their furniture, beds, and appliances. Now, mats on the floor serve as chairs, beds and tables. One bedroom has two hard, ratty couches and the other has a double bed that isn't much more than a thin mat on a precarious frame. Clothes are tucked neatly in suitcases. The kitchen is a sink, a propane hotplate and a small refrigerator. There is no garden here.

Abdullah brings out the girls' papers that we will take to the UN's makeshift warehouse to claim their "back-to-school" care packages: report cards and exclusive French-press passports, which are difficult to forge and, therefore, taken more seriously by countries considering resettlement.

While I thumb through the passports, Amina says she wasn't smiling in her photo because it was taken in Baghdad and she wasn't happy there. The sole stamp shows a border crossing last year, which the girls made specifically to get these valuable passports. Later this month, they will travel back to the border to get their visas renewed before they can start another year of Syrian school. If Abdullah didn't have children in school, he'd have to travel to the border to renew his visa every two months. It's a grueling bus trip that requires a twelve-hour day and costs about a week's salary. "It's all lines," Abdullah told me the first night we shared coffee in Damascus.

Abdullah and I try to decipher the girls' report cards, adorned with the official, ubiquitous photo of Syrian President Bashar Assad. I can (sort of) read the Arabic numbers of the grades. We start reading down through the subjects: Religion. English. ("Fourteen out of fifteen? You girls should be speaking English to me!" I say to widening eyes and vigorously shaking heads as their dad translates.)

French. ("French? I speak French! Ooh-la-la, escargot, chocolat. No, no, no, it's not 'bonjour.' It's 'booooon-jour,'" I sing, my voice rising like Mary Poppins on a springtime morning. "No, it's not 'je t'aime,'" I correct. "It's 'jhhhhe t'aime,'" I vamp over my shoulder, smoldering my glance and dropping my voice to Louie Armstrong octaves. The girls crack up.)

Science. "So are you as good as your father?" I challenge. He has studied animal husbandry and horticulture. The girls' enthusiasm spills over, trying to outdo each other in proving their scientific creds. They speak of microscopes and germs.

"Ask me anything!" Amina's smile widens, confident. Not knowing my germs, I punt, and explain that when I took biology in school, we dissected a worm. I illustrate their father's translations by scrunching my nose.

Amidst the girls' appreciative squealing, I tell them about dissecting a frog. I drop my head to the side, loll my tongue listlessly out of the corner of my mouth, feigning death, and limp-wrist my arms open, as if I were being dissected while Abdullah translates, running his index finger down his chest. Squeals broaden to laughter.

I tell them we dissected a baby pig, looking at the lungs, heart, stomach, and intestines, "and liver," adds Abdullah instructively.

"I saw a man die," Amina interrupts suddenly, her smile never leaving her face. Words spill out as I look on, smiling back, not understanding her Arabic story. When Abdullah finally translates, he shifts to that tight, detached jaw that I have come to know.

Amina had been out with her mother. They saw a man attacked by three other men with guns. They called the police to help the man, but he died.

This was the second time she had witnessed this.

It was the first time her father had heard this.

I lean over and kiss her forehead, more to hide my own emotion than to comfort this stoic child. It feels selfish to be more dramatic than everyone else in the room who had actually experienced these horrors. Amina had been twelve years old.

I feel like an intruder, interfering in this family, in this culture, in this shared Iraqi experience that I will never really know. Hope never to really know.

Abruptly shifting the mood, Abdullah announces it is time to go to the UN, and gathers the report cards and passports in a big envelope in his lap, his eyes overly intent on his work.

The girls' appointment, printed on watermarked paper to prevent forgery, is a two-hour block of time. We arrive a few minutes early and are ushered in with no fanfare by young staffers wearing large baby blue UN logos pinned to their T-shirts. As Abdullah secures the receipts, I head downstairs with the girls to a large room lined with overflowing mounds of school supplies: notebooks, shoes, jackets, pens, colored pencils. I expect the girls to brighten like Christmas morning, but they've been through this before.

We start at the backpack station. Amina and Lolou are each handed backpacks heavy enough to kill a strong mule. Twenty-six notepads of various sizes, pens, pencils, and a ruler. I am secretly envious; I have spent countless hours scouring Damascus for small, top spiral, cardboard backed notebooks in which to take my interview notes, only to receive regretful smiles from proprietors of dusty, cramped "stationery" nooks. I am in awe of the various notebook shapes, sizes, and cover artwork of the girls' new supplies.

As I thread the backpack straps through the tricky buckles so the girls can carry their new booty, I am approached by the same young Dane who'd escorted me from the food giveaway site. He asks me to leave and says I'm not authorized to be here. I explain I'm a family friend, and point to the girls being measured for their school uniforms, while clinging to the thick backpack strap I had just maneuvered through the buckle. "I'm here to help them carry their things." Abdullah looks blindsided, explaining that I'm "family." The young staffer is officious, forceful, and insists I'm not authorized to be here. Neither Abdullah nor I had been asked for ID at the front door.

Abdullah sets his jaw, preparing to negotiate, but I shake my head to stop him. As I walk toward the stairs to head outside, I overhear a woman working the check-out desk chastise the young man in English. Before I reach the stairway, the Dane apologizes, admitting there had been a mistake and that I could stay. Abdullah later tells me he thinks the woman worker is an Iraqi.

We were in and out in a record fifteen minutes. Abdullah couldn't believe it. Last year, they'd been there for hours. I still don't understand how this proud, accomplished, ambitious man who works two jobs under the table keeps his head up while standing in refugee lines for handouts.

Later that night, over *zataar*-spiced pizza and lemon-mint drinks, we review photos from my day's documentation of his day. He turns to me and says through that imperceptively expressive jaw, "I just want to live where I'm wanted."

One sultry night soon after, we stroll through one of Damascus' famous public gardens, the full moon bathing children swinging in the playground, still alive at 10:00 at night. Abdullah asks me to marry him.

He's always cared for me, he says, and he could start his life over with a green card.

I suspected a proposal might come, but until now I didn't know how I'd respond. I want to help, but standing in this fragrant, foreign garden I feel like an imposter, posing here as if I can really make a difference in this refugee tsunami. I start to cry.

And I say no.

Abdullah gives me a face-saving out by telling me he'd be happy just knowing I care about him. Sitting on a bench shadowed from the glances of the elderly women, we hold hands. I swipe my tears. We gaze at the Damascene moon. He kisses my wet cheek.

Later, I remember the parable of the beached starfish singled out by a little boy who, walking with his father, throws one of the hundreds of stranded starfish back into the sea. "What does it matter?" his father asks, gesturing to the litter of washed-up starfish.

"It mattered to that starfish," the boy points seaward.

And it mattered to that little boy, I've since come to realize.

The Happiest Place on Earth

[Disneyland]

Dina Kucera

Mom had never been on a vacation, ever. So we asked her, "If you could go anywhere, where would you go?"

She thought for a minute and then said, "Disneyland. I have never been to Disneyland." So we decided to take Mom to Disneyland.

We drive in two vehicles because we have to take Mom's toilet and her wheelchair. I shove them in the back of the Jeep, and it takes three people to push the door closed. Then we set out for Disneyland, the Happiest Place on Earth.

We make it to Los Angeles, but then we get lost for three hours. Every person in our caravan (me, Mom, my husband, my daughters, my grandson Moses) begins to melt down. I look out the window and notice the Burger King has bars on the windows.

We finally arrive at the hotel, exhausted, not one person speaking to another, except for the necessities: Someone bring in Grandma's toilet. Bed time. Go to hell. No, you go to hell.

After a good night's sleep, we all make up and drive across the street to the magic. It's time to go to Disneyland!

It seems like a thousand dollars later, but we are finally in. Mom is smiling. We are all smiling. This place is magic! It is almost 100 degrees, but that is okay. Everything is glittering and colorful.

I push Mom through the gate and say, "Here we go, Mom! We're at Disneyland!"

I get about ten feet when Mom's wheelchair very abruptly stops and lurches forward, almost hurling her out onto the golden brick road. I look down. Tracks. There are train tracks? I look ahead and realize there are train tracks everywhere. To get Mom's wheelchair over them, we all have to lift her so the wheels don't get wedged in the track. John and I look at each other and without saying a word, we know we have just entered hell.

Every few feet we lift, push for a few seconds, and then lift again. We are lifting the wheelchair with Mom in it when we hear the trolley making its way around the track. In the nick of time, we get Mom off the track, and the trolley passes with smiling people waving and having the time of their lives. John and I stare at them with sweat rolling down our faces.

The lines for the magic rides are about forty minutes. I understand why they sell three-day passes now. If you want to ride several of the rides, it will take three days.

By lunchtime, Moses' face is beet red. Mom is also getting sunburned. I slather both of them with sun block, just as I had done before we left. We are sitting in some sort of fairy restaurant after waiting for more than an hour. Moses refuses to eat. I tell him to eat his fairy burger. He has a screaming attack right in front of all the fairies. Then April begins to lose it, and then I begin to lose it, and we don't give a shit what the fairies are thinking. One hundred thirty-six dollars later, lunch is over. The fairies are not sorry to see us leave.

We go back out to the mean streets of Disneyland. The fun Disney characters are everywhere. Moses does not appreciate them one little bit. He cries every time one comes close to us. I try to wave them off, but they come anyway. Moses screams. I smile and tell the characters they are doing a great job.

The characters don't talk. They just do fun, silly body movements. I raise my hand to stop them, and they put their hands on their enormous bellies as if they are laughing and walk away in their giant outfits.

Mom wants to go on a ride, but the only ride in the magic kingdom that Mom can go on is "It's a Small World."

Because Mom is in a wheelchair—and because God had mercy on us—we don't have to wait in line. The entire family goes on the ride. We enter the tunnel, and immediately we are hit with the most beautiful cool air. We all realize our day just got better.

It turns out the world is not as small as you might have thought. The ride goes on forever, which is great. It is a fun ride with all the different countries and the music and air conditioning.

We come back out of the tunnel and pull up to the ride guy. We begin to stand and he says, "Wanna go again?"

We all look at each other, confused. Mom says, "Yes! We do!" So off we go, back into the air-conditioned tunnel.

Four times. We go through four times. That's how long it takes to lower our body temperatures to an almost normal level.

Afterwards, I am desperately looking for a tree to park Mom under. I find one tree. There are about sixteen Japanese people standing under it. They look like they are wedged into a crowded elevator. Each of them has a camera hanging from his neck. There is no way in.

We all have first degree burns. I stand in line for half an hour to get water. Some to drink and some to dump on my family members' heads to save their lives. Nineteen dollars later, I get the water. Moses is bright red and crying in that miserable way that children cry when they have really had enough—sobbing, snot running out of his nose, rubbing his eyes. I am leaning down, patting Moses' back, saying, "It's okay, Sweetie. I know, I know…" when I see two enormous brown furry feet step into our space. I look up. It is another giant cartoon character. He waves. I say, "Please. Step away from the child."

The character does the same hand-on-the-belly laughing thing as all the other characters and shuffles away.

I look at my family, and I can sense that the big people could actually have some fun if they didn't have to worry about lugging around a tired, sunburned baby and an old lady in a wheelchair. I tell John to take us back to the room. And trust me, it is no sacrifice on my part.

Mom and Moses and I get back into our room and it is truly magical. We crank up the air, order room service, strip down to our underwear, and climb in the big beautiful bed. We are all thrilled. We eat cheeseburgers and drink chocolate shakes and watch TV. It is the best part of the trip. The three of us fall asleep for about three hours with the nice air conditioning blowing on our sunburned skin. Aaaah…life is great.

The others stay at Disneyland until late into the night, which is wonderful. They call several times saying, "Are you guys ready to come back?"

I look at Moses sitting in his bath playing so peacefully, and Mom eating ice cream and watching something on TV. I say, "I don't think so. Really, we are fine."

Later in the evening, Moses and I take a walk and go swimming. It is nice and calm and fun.

I put Mom to bed in her little bedroom attached to our room. I am covering her and notice her window shade is open. Outside her window you can see Disneyland. Right at that moment, they begin a fireworks show.

I say, "Look, Mom. Fireworks!"

She watches as she lies in her bed. I call Moses in and he jumps up on the bed between me and Mom. Moses is pointing and smiling. Mom is smiling. There is complete silence…just beautiful, brilliant flashes of light and color filling the sky. The three of us lie there, hypnotized, each explosion greater than the last, and sometimes it feels like the fireworks are coming down on top of us. I look over at my mom. She looks happy. It seems like this is what she came for. The show goes on for about twenty minutes, and we watch all the way through.

When it is over, I close the shade, and pull the blanket over Mom's shoulders.

She says, "That was the best fireworks show I've ever seen."

I say, "Me too."

Right at that moment, I feel a connection to my mother that I have not felt in years. It is me and my mom watching the fireworks. It feels like we are both present for the first time in a long, long time. It is a moment I will never forget. It is magical.

I don't think moments are the things in life we plan. Like getting married or having children. Genuine moments happen when you aren't expecting them. Those are the things you remember all your life. Little snapshots that you can see as if they just happened. I went to bed grateful for that little bit of time with my mom, and I remembered just for a second what she used to be like.

We got home and it took six weeks to heal from the effects of Disneyland. We put the toilet back in Mom's bathroom and unloaded her wheelchair. I was happy Mom went to Disneyland, and she has an eighteen dollar coffee cup to prove she was there.

People always say, "You have to go to Disneyland. At least once." I agree. You have to go. At least once. But you know where the happiest place on Earth is? My house. My bed. It turns out the best part of going to Disneyland is coming home.

Berlin
[Germany]

Jennifer Lang

We met the young woman in the hallway of a school in Berlin. My mom and I were talking to the history teacher when the woman whisked by. With a black leather briefcase slung over one shoulder and another two bags in her hands, she skirted around us.

"Slicha," she said, racing up the stairs as if being chased by a swarm of bees. It surprised me to hear that familiar Hebrew word for "excuse me" in Berlin. I looked at my mom.

"Did you hear that?" I whispered. Neither of us wanted to be boorish and interrupt the history teacher, who, in faltering English, was translating the German plaque for us—how many Jewish girls had been deported from this school, how many Jewish boys from another neighborhood school and when. My mom and I glanced at the top of the stairs. The woman stopped briefly and stared back at us.

"Did you say something in Hebrew?" my mom asked her. The woman nodded. "But why?" The diminutive woman with a perfect brown bob darted back down to the landing. She and the history teacher smiled at one another, and then the history teacher left, wishing us a good visit.

"My grandmother was Jewish," said the woman. "I know a few words in Hebrew." She had assumed we were Jewish and would understand since she had seen us talking with her colleague about the deportations. "I am the English and music teacher here and music director for all Berlin schools. I just came from the Bundestag, the government, and am in a hurry to get ready for my next class. Sorry." I was impressed. Her English was fluent, despite the accent, and she seemed to have an important role in the school system. "I just finished working on a piece that Schoenberg wrote. You've heard of him, yes? He wrote a seven-minute song called "A Survivor of Warsaw" based on a diary from someone in the ghetto."

I couldn't tell her age, perhaps in her late forties or early fifties. Like a field mouse, this woman was exceptionally fast. Everything about her was quick—her thoughts, her speech, her gestures, her gait.

"So, you understood the plaque?" she asked, turning her attention back to the wall, the reason we were in the building. We nodded, not wanting to keep her long but interested in her story. "I have an idea," she continued. She dashed back up the stairs and motioned swiftly for us to follow since, she said, the bell was going to ring and hundreds of hurried students were going to pour into the stairwell. "Can you come to my next class and talk with the children? So they can hear your English and practice theirs? It starts in ten minutes. We just first go to the teachers' lounge so I get ready."

Mom and I looked at each other and shrugged our shoulders in agreement. It was our last day in Berlin. In the past five days we had checked off everything on our list—art museums, memorials, Sachsenhausen concentration camp, Europe's oldest Jewish cemetery, the Stasi secret police headquarters, the Reichstag. I had even squeezed in two yoga classes, in German. "Gut!" she said, indicating for us to follow her down the hallway. This woman captivated us.

My mom and I had come from opposite ends of the globe—she from California and I from Israel, where my family was spending the year—but our goals were similar. We wanted to see as much modern art and war-related and Eastern bloc history as possible. Knowing that Berlin was the headquarters for Nazi Germany, we wanted to see firsthand the remnants of World War II. Like many Jews today, we fear that the atrocities committed during the Holocaust may one day be forgotten. Even though our family had left Europe long before the war, we were each drawn to the history and to personal stories we had been hearing for most of our lives. With that in mind, my mom had hired Thorsten, a private guide, to talk to us and take us to out-of-the-way places for a day.

A Ph.D. student in Jewish History and Holocaust Studies, Thorsten wasn't Jewish and had entered the field because of his own family history. His father grew up in Denmark with German parents who were nationalistic and supportive of the Nazi regime, while his mother hailed from an ethnically Danish family who were German citizens and anti-Nazi. Raised in Denmark, Thorsten spent the year after university in Jerusalem and then, at age nineteen, moved to Germany. As an adult, he believed that to confront and accept his dual identity, he had to come to terms with his grandparents' choices and connect to both countries' pasts.

As we drove from memorial to memorial, this tall, handsome man with his melodious voice recounted their meanings and origins—if erected by a local group of nuns, a grassroots neighborhood association or the residents, whether vandalized or well-preserved. If Thorsten hadn't accompanied us and shared his wealth of knowledge surrounding the memorials, my mom and I probably wouldn't have seen or understood the importance or meaning behind many of them. By the day's end, we had visited six, one more powerful than the next.

On our last day, my mother and I decided to forgo another museum and instead search for two off-the-beaten-path memorials that Thorsten had mentioned. The first was in the middle of a square, a few feet from the U-bahn station Rathaus Steglitz, where a weekend market is held. Called "Mirrored Wall," it had thousands of names of Jews who were deported from that neighborhood. In it, we could see ourselves, as well as the rest of the world walking or biking or driving by. Taxis still honked and people still talked.

The second memorial was in an upscale, residential neighborhood and enormous. It bordered on a playground and jutted out into the sidewalk. Towering over us was a wall with names and dates of transports, and alongside was an old steel boxcar with cement bodies huddled together as if trapped inside. Even though Thorsten had described them to us, we had forgotten their significance and were frustrated by the lack of signage.

Curious, we asked three girls walking by if they knew about the monuments and could explain. Though all were of Turkish origin, one was more fluent in English and became the designated spokesperson.

"I am old, very old, twenty-one, and when I was younger I go to the school nearby," she explained, pointing her finger at a building down the road. Her light-hearted grin turned serious. "It was a girls' Jewish school. The memorials here show where these girls went, the camp names and the dates, you see." We looked up in the bright spring sun. Most were sent to Auschwitz or Theresiendstadt.

"How do you know this?" I asked. My desire to understand what Berliners think—of us, of Jews, of the country's past—was like chicken pox, a deep, endless itch.

"From my teachers. Every year they teach us what happened so we remember, so it never happen again." She was eleven when she first learned about the Holocaust. "You can visit the school to see inside," she said. "There is explanation on wall."

Following her suggestion, we entered the quiet school building a little after noon. We peeked around and found the plaque on the landing of the stairway leading to the classrooms. Since it was written in German, we stopped a man, who turned out to be the history teacher, and asked if he could help us. After explaining it word for word, he lumbered back upstairs to fetch a copy of a newsletter he had written about the previous year's Holocaust program at the school, held every year on November 9. On that day in 1918 the country proclaimed its first democracy. Then, on that same day in 1938, came Kristallnacht, the night of broken glass when violence against Jews in Germany escalated. And on the ninth in 1989, the Berlin Wall came down. He pointed out the front-page picture of now ninety-one-year-old Lolita Goldstein, who was saved by the headmaster when all the other girls were being rounded up, and who comes every June from Manhattan to tell her story to the high school students.

That's when the English teacher whisked by.

Once seated in the faculty lounge before class, the English teacher extended her right arm.

"I'm Claire Hermann," she said, pumping my hand up and down and then my mom's. Even though she was extremely petite, her handshake was strong. She inhaled a deep, long breath and on the exhale, spoke nonstop, summing up the story she had started on the stairs about her grandmother. As an adult, Frau Hermann had learned that part of her family had come from a line of Orthodox rabbis in Germany and another part had been baptized. Her Jewish grandmother had married a Protestant reverend, and they had four children. During the war, they tried to protect them by hiding their Jewish identity, sending one to France, one to an elite Nazi boarding school, and one to live with friends. The fourth wasn't as fortunate and ended up in a forced labor camp, where he died. Only six years ago had the teacher discovered her family history while visiting the Jewish Museum in Berlin, where she saw the name of the camp where her uncle was killed. For the first time, she put the information together, realizing he was Jewish. Since then, she has made several trips to Israel to learn more about her family at the Yad Vashem Holocaust Martyrs' and Heroes' Remembrance Authority in Jerusalem.

A bell rang. The teacher hoisted her bags over her shoulders, waving us to walk down the hall. She warned us the kids were noisy and apologized beforehand for any misconduct. By the time we entered the room, everyone was seated. The walls were bare: no posters, diagrams, or maps. Boys and girls were sitting in rows of two, three, and four at long tables. They looked older, tougher than their fourteen years. Frau Hermann pulled up the only two extra chairs for my mom and me to sit in the front of the class.

Clap of the hands. Clearing of the throat. Cluck of the tongue. Standing, she took charge, quieting the room. Papers rustled, kids whispered, chairs slid on the linoleum floor.

"We have some special visitors today," she began in English, repeating certain parts in German to make sure they understood, telling them how we had met. She asked us to introduce ourselves and then picked certain kids to introduce themselves—a boy born of Sri Lankan parents, one from Vietnam, another from Poland, and a girl from Turkey. With a show of hands, we learned that all twenty-seven of them were born in Berlin, but only five had German-born parents. Of the foreigners, the majority were Turkish. Two-thirds of the class was Muslim.

Then Frau Hermann instructed them to ask us questions. "Was San Francisco pretty?" one boy asked my mom. "Why did my family want to live in Israel?" another asked me. "Was it dangerous?" We answered slowly, choosing our words carefully.

The conversation turned to values: which ones were important to us, to them, and why. I couldn't hold my tongue. That deep-down itch had flared up again. I asked if we could discuss what led us into that room.

Cluck of the tongue. Clearing of the throat. Frau Hermann regained control over the cacophony of kids and then turned the floor over to me.

"When you walk by a memorial on the street, do you think about what it is? Do you think there are too many memorials in Berlin?" I paused. "Is the story of the Holocaust in the media too much? Is it important to learn about it and remember?" I had lumped too many questions together but wanted to unleash them from within. Throughout the past few days, as my mother and I viewed memorials, these questions had simmered inside me.

The teacher nodded her head as if to approve and opened them up for discussion. "Who can answer?"

A blond girl in the back of the room raised her hand. "It's good to remember because it's our history. We can't escape it. We should know so it doesn't happen again."

"Even if my parents not born here, I live in Germany. I must know history," another boy chimed in.

I wondered about those whose families were German. "Do you know your family's story, if your family is from here?" I asked.

"My grandfather was Nazi officer and got medals during the war. But my grandmother hated it and throw them in the bin," said a dark-haired girl with a pierced nose. I got goose bumps.

A hand went up in the front row. "My great-grandmother was Bulgarian," said a burly blond-headed boy.

"During the war, she escape back to Bulgaria, then Turkey, and after the war back here. She left Germany because she was foreigner with dark hair." He looked me straight in the eyes. "We learn about it in history," he said, handing me their book. There was page after page on Hitler's rise to power with pictures of the yellow Juden star on clothes and heaps of dead bodies being buried in the camps. While we couldn't read or understand the words, the images said a lot. Germany is reckoning with its past in every way it can.

The bell rang, bringing a sudden close to the conversation. The students packed up to leave. Neither my mother nor I were ready for the give-and-take to end. Speechless, we smiled at the room of strangers. Two kids stopped to thank us. One asked if they could do this again. We thanked them back, but I'm not sure they understood.

Frau Hermann led us back to the teachers' lounge for a glass of water and to decompress. She was very appreciative of our time, telling us over and over how important it was for the students to hear English spoken by native speakers. But we knew that more had transpired in that class than a foreign language lesson.

A Quick and Cozy Kidnapping
[Nicaragua]

Ben Bellizzi

There's something to be said for the unique reaction triggered in a person who has been threatened with an unconventional weapon. Whereas a pointed gun elicits no mystery as to the holder's intentions, and little more with a wielded knife, the use of an everyday tool as a means to bring about harm allows one's imagination to run wild with the possibilities of how that pain may be inflicted. In this particular case, as I was trapped in the backseat of a taxi, my limbs pinned down beneath the weight of my fellow passengers while we meandered through the dirt roads of a remote area of Nicaragua, it was a flat-headed screwdriver poised above my left kneecap that sparked my imagination and persuaded me to comply with any requests. While a flat-headed screwdriver may not even be considered the more treacherous of the two types of screwdrivers, its position hovering over the kneecap transformed it into a monster. Anyone who's ever banged a knee into a desk leg or a metal pole can attest to the fact that it hurts like the dickens, and whether the woman holding the weapon meant to bore it into my skin, or to slash at the area, or just to whack the hell out of it with the handle, I was not eager to discover.

The reality that this tool was apparently the most effective weapon at the group's disposal spoke volumes as to their desperation. Regardless of whether their tactics were born out of psychological intuition or of necessity, I may now declare their attempts to instill fear a rousing success, for in my stuttering, rudimentary Spanish, I surrendered the pin number to my ATM card without further hesitation.

Years later, I remain puzzled. On one steamy day in Central America, sitting quietly on a converted school bus, anticipating the pleasures of a much needed shower, I somehow came to be the target of a relatively intricate plot to extract money from a gringo tourist entering Nicaragua via the Costa Rican border. My bags were old and worn, my clothes riddled with dust, and though everything about me must have reeked of exhaustion, I was an able-bodied, reasonably-sized male in my mid-twenties. If my mind hadn't become so taken with the deviant uses of a screwdriver, I was apt to put up enough of a struggle to make a mess of the backseat of any compact car. Perhaps it was my black computer bag that first prompted the squat woman with the hard, beady eyes to deem me as valuable. Perhaps it was my blue jeans or nothing more than my white skin. Whatever the reason, this woman's first move was to flash me a smile that conveyed neither warmth nor kindness, and when she asked that I pile my bags on my lap so that she might occupy the seat beside me instead of the several other vacant ones, she stifled all breathable air lingering in the midday heat. I disliked her immediately.

Once the bus started moving, the woman made strained and somewhat crass appeals for friendship. Her touching of my arm and unnecessary rises in intonation irritated me along with her convenient discovery that we were headed for the same destination. I had no phone number to give her, was reluctant to exchange e-mail addresses, and I would have been happy to rid myself of her at the first possible opportunity except that I suspected myself of dismissing her largely on account of her harsh physicality. She was unattractive in just about every way. Even her words, spoken in order to convey warmth, came off as ugly.

My aversion, however, managed to work in her favor. One of the goals of my travels was to initiate certain improvements in my own character, and at the time I was inclined to believe myself guilty of a substantial amount of vanity. It's quite natural to want to befriend people who are physically handsome, yet when I reviewed my friends and found not a single troll among them, I worried that their looks, more than anything else, might have dictated the terms of our primary engagements. As a result, I began to consider how I might have approached this present woman's calls for friendship had she been something more to look at. I felt certain that, as I was traveling alone, I would have been prone to seeking the companionship of a foreign seductress. In fact, it was one of the more ambitious goals of my trip. Once admitting this, I felt disgraced, and so with an eye toward righting my moral compass, I succumbed to guilt and agreed to share an eastbound taxi with this unfortunate woman to the city of Granada. So proud was I of my grand swing in ethics that I failed to become alarmed when two additional people casually entered the taxi. They surrounded me in the middle of the backseat, moving in a way that displayed a vast amount of unspoken communication, and the vehicle swung left and to the north while I congratulated myself for my superior sense of humanity. All was well in that silent taxi, for as a stranger in a strange land, I stumbled upon oddities around just about every corner. At one point I did entertain the thought that if ever I were to be robbed, I was now planted in the ideal situation, but I quickly discarded the notion as holding no water. It would have been callous of me to resort to cynicism, and lost in both language and landscape, it's often best to simply play along.

Half an hour later I'd surrendered my cash and my bank card, squealed out my pin number, and was pleading to retain my passport. Yet the taxi's occupants ignored the document and yelled repeatedly, "We want your monies! More monies!" Cringing at their grammar (being the son of an English teacher, the unnecessary "s" was simply infuriating), I neglected to correct their error in language and assured them that they had everything I could possibly give them. I explained how my bank only allowed me to extract a set amount each day, how it was impossible even for me personally to take out more, and it was around this time, when the payoff of their labor showed signs of falling short of their projections, that the dynamics of the group presented themselves.

My captor (I hesitate to say seductress) sat on my left. I can only guess from what soon played out that her brother drove, his wife rode beside him, and in the backseat on my right was perhaps a cousin, a quiet soul with no stomach for such an operation. The pair in the front was certainly married in their desire for a hefty score. Yet once we dropped off the wife at an ATM and returned to the back roads, it became evident that the two in the rear seats were much more prone to compassion than those in the front. An argument arose between the driver and my captor when I pleaded to retain my computer, for I claimed (not untruthfully) that it was very old, barely functional, and contained every bit of work I'd ever done. I told them I was in their country to work, I needed my computer to do so, and they should be able to tell from my bag full of dirty socks that I was a student and had little money. (Again I considered highlighting the correct use of the irregular plural, but again, I abstained.)

My captor rooted through my bag with an expression somewhere between disgust and pity. She examined the gas station-purchased disposable camera and the frayed underwear that would have sent my mother on a b-line to Macy's, and then agreed with my financial appraisal. The woman argued the case to her brother, and along with the cousin on my right, she began to caress my hands as opposed to pinning them. As I shook with nerves, I appreciated their unexpected support and found their touches soothing.

Meanwhile, my captor and her brother screamed at each other like only family can. I interjected once on my behalf, but my captor turned her hard, beady eyes on me and told me to be quiet. Her brother wanted to shoot me. I didn't at all believe he had a gun, but I did believe he would have liked to shoot me. Since he likely lacked the means to do so, I wondered how he might take out his multiple frustrations with a flat-headed screwdriver. Regardless, it was clear to me that this was a family squabble and it was best for everybody if I stayed out of the way.

When we picked up the wife from the ATM, the conflict came to a head. The two in front were furious at the meager amount they had procured while the two in back saw the disappointment as evidence of my humble position. They pointed their fingers across seats, at my computer, into the rear and side-view mirrors, and meanwhile the quiet cousin had progressed to tears. She was either unable or unwilling to contain her emotions and she demanded they stop the car. As we slowed to the side of the road, I thought of how the scene was not too distant from the ill-fated vacations my family insisted on undertaking each summer: an argument escalating on all sides, someone threatening to exit the vehicle, and me in the middle of the backseat, scared, confused, and unsure of what was to ensue. We even seemed to be lost.

I waited patiently beside the open door as the cousin composed herself. Escape did not occur to me. I was invested in a family argument and one faction was depending on me; to try to leave then would have meant betrayal. It was safer to stay. When the cousin returned to the car I took up her hand in mine and did my best to comfort her.

As we drove away, a final riff erupted concerning the computer. I now viewed the world outside the car as one I might return to, and after an hour and a half it seemed possible that, barring any major blunders, I might get away with my computer after all. I quietly supported those arguing in my favor, though I got the feeling that all four just wanted me gone so they could really get after each other. The two in front demanded the computer more for reparations than for worth, but my captor fought tenaciously for me. Those hard eyes of hers were ready for anything the opposition could throw at her, and when she'd finally prevailed, she turned to me, pressed the computer to my chest, and looked upon me in an almost motherly fashion. I froze and stared at her like a child. We gazed at each other, the car and its passengers and everything else around us melting away, and in that fantastically serene moment, free from noise or heat or dust, I watched her eyes soften. They were tired and apologetic, longing to communicate so much more than our situation allowed, and they squinted in a pained manner, as if to say, "I'm sorry I had to rob you." I nodded in understanding and squinted back, "I'm sorry I have so little for you to rob," hoping that she didn't catch me gazing longingly through the window behind her. I blinked, and in an instant the noise and the heat and the dust returned. She helped me zip up my bag, though she paused to allow her sister-in-law to relieve me of my electric razor. Family always comes first. I tried to appear sad and make the wife feel as if she'd won something, for the razor was heavy and finicky and surely could have done a number on my kneecap.

After receiving my maxed-out ATM card, I successfully lobbied for twenty dollars of my own money so that I might pay for a bus to my original destination. The sister-in-law refused, but my captor insisted. I was on a bit of a roll and thought of asking for more, but I didn't press my luck.

They left me by the side of the highway on the outskirts of Managua, flustered but free, and more than anything, thankful that the screwdriver had not been corrupted into violence. I stood there as they sped off, thinking nothing of catching a glimpse of their license plate, but rather of the tear-dampened hand belonging to the woman on my right and of the hard, beady eyes belonging to the woman on my left. I still remember those eyes, still remember the fear they incited in me, but I also remember that with a touch of patience and a series of events that I can only describe as familial, they somehow came to soften.

Turbulence
[On the plane]

Roz Warren

You don't expect trouble from a librarian. We try to avoid problems. We plan ahead. That's why I always request a seat assignment when I make a plane reservation instead of waiting until I get to the airport. I ask for a window seat in a two-seat row near the front.

Of course, things don't always go according to plan. I've arrived at the terminal to find I've been given another seat, or that my flight has been cancelled entirely. Once we couldn't take off for hours because, according to the flight attendant, we were waiting for a kidney in a cooler to arrive on a connecting flight from Cincinnati. That took so long that I missed my own connecting flight and I had to wait half a day in Atlanta for another one. But somebody waiting on an operating table that day got a kidney, so I was okay with that.

Today I'm one of the first to board and am delighted to see I have just what I want—a window seat with just one seat beside it. I put my purse on the seat and go to the bathroom. When I return, there's a little boy sitting in my seat. A plump woman with short brown hair sits next to him.

My heart sinks. Everyone knows mothers and their children shouldn't be separated while traveling—except the airlines, who do it all the time. I'm guessing this woman has been seated next to me, while her child has been seated in an entirely different section of the plane.

I hover in the aisle for a moment. When she spots me, she thrusts two boarding passes at me, for seats 23B and 26E. "Bobby and I aren't together," she says flatly. "Can we switch seats?"

I'm about to hand over my precious boarding pass when it strikes me: neither 23B nor 26E are anywhere near these seats! Bobby and Mom have no claim whatsoever to the seats they're sitting in. When you and your child are seated apart, you're supposed to ask the person sitting next to your child to switch with you. But Bobby's mom has taken the opportunity to do a little seat shopping. She spotted these two and figured she could grab them.

I'm both impressed and dismayed by her chutzpah. She waves the boarding passes at me with barely a glance in my direction. She doesn't expect me to put up a fight for my seat. I don't look like a fighter. I look like what I am—a librarian. Nobody is intimidated by a librarian.

You never hear anyone say, "She's got a masters in library science—watch out!"

We librarians are terminally helpful. Nice as can be. People-pleasers.

But even we know there's a line between being pleasantly accommodating and being a doormat. And I believe that I'm looking at it right now. Summoning up all my courage, I clear my throat.

She glances up, startled. Our eyes meet.

"Is either of the seats you're offering me a window seat?" I ask.

She eyes me suspiciously. "A window seat?"

"The two seats that you've been assigned—neither of which you're sitting in, obviously—is either seat next to a window?"

"A window? No."

"Then I believe I'll sit in my own seat, thank you."

"You mean you won't switch with me?" she demands. Her voice shrill.

"I'm terribly sorry, but you're going to have to ask the person seated next to your son to trade seats with you."

I really am terribly sorry. There's nothing more harrowing for a people-pleaser than making another person really angry. Which is what I've just done. She glares at me, then grabs Bobby's arm and yanks him from my seat. "C'mon," she huffs. "This lady refuses to help us!"

I reclaim my seat, my heart racing. The plane hasn't even left the tarmac and I've already experienced way too much turbulence.

If the plane crashes, will I regret having been so petty?

Know what? I don't think so.

I'm gazing out the window when someone finally arrives to take the seat beside mine—a little girl, hugging a stuffed tiger. Close behind is her mother.

"I'm terribly sorry," Mom says, "but Lydia has been assigned this seat and I'm supposed to sit three rows back. Would you mind terribly if…"

"Of course not." With a reassuring smile, I hand over my boarding pass and go off in search of my new seat, knowing that if we do go down, I've somehow managed to be, after all, a nice helpful librarian.

Encounter
[Alaska]

Shannon Huffman Polson

The last long trip my husband, Peter, and I took together before the baby was also the first time either of us had been to the Western Arctic. We set up camp in the far northwestern corner of Alaska, accessible only by an hour-and-a-half flight on a Beaver de Havilland from the closest road in the outpost of Coldfoot, Alaska. Our first day on the banks of the narrow, serpentine Nigu River, we left to explore the foothills of the mountains just beyond our tent. A cool east wind blew. I was four-and-a-half months pregnant, and my belly was too big to zip up my rain parka, so I wore it open. With each step, the uneven tundra humbled me, along with my diminishing muscle and lung capacity. My body had its own agenda now, and I was not first priority. Peter slung the steel 12-gauge loaded with slugs over his shoulder. Both of us carried bear spray on the belts of our daypacks.

We knew as we began our hike that it was unlikely we would see much wildlife at all, other than the scattered groups of caribou beginning to make their way south and the occasional ground squirrel. We heard wolves howl within an hour of arriving in this wild space, but to see a wolf is uncommon. Barren-ground grizzlies require a great deal of land to roam. Food is scarce. Each travels great distances in a day in his search for sustenance, and perhaps impatient with this requirement, is more aggressive than a grizzly living to the south where food supplies are more plentiful. Still, his diet is almost exclusively plant based, long claws developed for digging roots and berries. Because of his large range, he is a rarity as well. The shotgun and bear spray we brought with us were merely precautions.

Fast moving weather played across the Arctic amphitheater, alternately shining swaths of soft sunlight across smooth verdant hillsides, quickly swallowed by dark clouds emerging to spatter rain which, within tens of minutes, was replaced again by scattered sunlight. Deep grey clouds clinging to the mountains to our south lit up with a rainbow. The clean lines of landscape outlined a stage upon which creation entire played.

Not more than fifteen minutes from camp, heading up a nearby foothill, Peter stopped and pointed at the middle of the hill.

"What's that?"

Our inquiries to one another on any number of hikes resulted in the careful observation of what would typically turn out to be a serenely settled boulder. I squinted at the hill, the tundra green in the short summer, small deeper green copses of dwarf-birch and willow. This time the boulder moved.

"Grizzly," I said. "He's huge. He's coming right at us—and we're downwind." I spoke as though exposition might somehow distance the danger. "He can't see us yet, either." The river bordered us to our right, and the mountain soared up to our left. The grizzly was coming down the mountain on the most sensible path, which happened to be the one we were also following, each toward the other.

The bear moved forward. His head was down, highlighting the telltale hump of the grizzly, the genetic adaptation of bone and muscle between his massive shoulders to help with digging and quick bursts of speed in pursuit of prey. Though seemingly unhurried, he covered ground quickly. Even at a distance, his thick tawny coat rippled like the cape of a king. Power emanating from each of his movements pulsed in the air around him. I fancied the hill quaking under his feet, the tundra bowing down before him. I would have happily bowed along with it—inside I did—but it violated the general principles of "look big, stay stationary, and talk or yell loudly." Despite my internal genuflections to His Majesty, I hoped for a distant and respectful meeting.

Peter and I waved our trekking poles over our heads. "He-llo! He-llo!" we yelled into the wind. It felt futile. How would he ever hear us? How close would he need to get?

Undeterred, mostly because we did not have another option, we continued to yell. Native Americans believe that bear always knows when you talk about him, and could be angered, so out of respect they never mention him by name.

They will call him other names: brother, grandmother, but never bear. So we continued to simply greet the rapid advance. Our feet remained anchored, though my heart sprinted away. I pulled out my bear spray and unclipped the locking mechanism. The wind direction did not favor its deployment.

Then he stopped, still a distance away, a slow, rolling halt. He stood up on his hind legs, tall, immense, his powerful front legs, strong enough to decapitate an animal in a single blow, hanging at his sides like arms. As he stood, for just a moment, my lungs emptied involuntarily. I stopped yelling, and rested my hand gently on my belly. A prayer.

"He's beautiful," I whispered to Peter.

Have you ever had a grizzly consider you closely? The previous summer we had watched a grizzly from a similar distance moving away from us. One's perspective on a grizzly moving directly toward you is considerably different. There is little else in life to so thoroughly convince you, in an instant, of the naked vulnerability of mere humanity. What must he have thought of two brightly colored fleece and Gore-tex clad two-legged creatures standing in his path? What furnace of wildness roiled in him? What internal urge propelled him over this mountain, at this time?

It was an animal just like this—a healthy, male, barren-ground grizzly—that four years ago killed my father and stepmother, coming into their camp a few hundred miles east of where we stood, perhaps surprised and reacting in fear, perhaps acting on his predatory nature. The attack was unprecedented and inexplicable, even to wildlife biologists. My dad and stepmom traveled to the Arctic for its remote beauty. I followed them to the Arctic to understand the peace that only the purity of true wilderness can bring, even in the wake of its cruelty. But either way, he killed them—violently, quickly—and I lost them forever. The bear followed them into the other world just as quickly when the authorities dropped him the next day with four shotgun slugs through the chest. Killing is not left only to animals.

I suppose I'd been waiting for this meeting for some time. This was my third trip to the Arctic since the bear and two of the people I loved most intersected on their fatal paths. Each time I came expecting a meeting. My first trip, embarking with a sophomoric and absurd defiance born of terror and mitigated only by remnants of numbness, I saw no sign at all. On my second trip, a healthy respect still tinged with fear walked with me. Numerous healthy piles of fresh scat and aggressive, extensive diggings told me of grizzly's presence, but he never showed his face. This trip there had been no scat, no digging, only a few pigeon-toed human-like prints on the sandy beaches, bordered on the front with the distinctive deep punctures of the grizzly's long claws.

This physical similarity of bear to humans in footprint and stature, along with the hibernation-like slumber and protracted nurturing of young, has captivated people from the beginning of time. Circumpolar peoples for tens of thousands of years have remarkably intricate and similar ceremonies around the killing of bear, and cave paintings and skeletal arrangements show evidence of bear cults as long ago as 30,000 years. In most native cultures, bear either is a god himself, or at the very least an interlocutor with the gods. Many native ceremonies for initiation into secret societies or shamanism involve bear, reduction of the initiate to nothing and reconstitution to new life. Humans and bear compete for similar resources. Bear encouraged the formation of human communities, which bonded to protect themselves from bear and other predators. From the earliest humans, we and bear have been inextricably linked, body and soul.

Watching him standing there on the tundra, looking at me, smelling the air, I suddenly saw him not only as the other, not only as the wild, the powerful, the terrifying, but as myself. How often did I move forward, head down, and coming across something I didn't understand, stand, arms dangling, and sniff the air? If this King of the Arctic sometimes reacted with violence, how often did I, out of fear or anger, lash out and destroy everything in my path, or retreat covered in blood and bruises? Looking at him standing there on the tundra, I was startled. I was scared because I saw myself in him. And I loved him for the same reason. We were of different worlds, and yet we were not so different. Watching him, a piece of memory I had never known unrolled in front of me. Color painted onto image. Beauty drawn onto a recollection of pain.

Peter gazed on evenly with awe. It is how Peter considers most things. I envied him that. I fingered the smooth top of the nozzle on the bear spray, which felt inadequate, and even absurd.

The grizzly remained on his hind legs, towering, still, his small eyes peering in our direction, huge head tilted to sniff the air. We stood waving poles and hollering. In the chess game of wilderness, only he knew the rules. The next move was entirely his. We would have to try to understand with a quick interpretation. This was his land, his game. He only took a half-minute to consider. Turning a darker brown bottom to us, he bounded back up and over the mountain from where he had come, long strong bounds, covering great distances, so that it took him only perhaps a minute to ascend the hill and disappear over the other side. Why in the world he would turn and run from us still baffles me. Perhaps looking at us, he saw himself, too.

I had envisioned a meeting with grizzly. He sauntered toward me and stopped, knowing that somehow he owed me one. He looked at me with confusion or surprise, but he knew. He knew and he turned away.

My visions were of course ridiculous. There is no mercy or fairness in the wild. There is only untamed innocence. And in that there are no guarantees. My reaction demonstrated this: I froze. I did not rationally consider anything. But no matter. My shortcomings notwithstanding, I had been expecting him. We had to meet.

Our meeting marked far more than merely satisfying my sense of eventual inevitability. To encounter a grizzly was to rendezvous with no less than the creation which formed and still today forms these ancient lands. Grizzly, as the other large predator, is an indicator of the completeness and complexity of the Arctic eco-system. The Arctic is the last great wild space in which they can thrive. I was face-to-face with creation. I was in and of creation.

That night we crawled into our sleeping bag, zipping up the tent behind us. Outside a set of thin wires carrying an electric current surrounded the tent to discourage any larger visitors. While the wild offers no assurances, we can take precautions. I lay down and snuggled against Peter, hiding in the comforting curve of his body. His arm draped across me, and his hand rested on my protruding belly. I felt his breath in my hair and against my neck. I looked through the mesh wall at the bottom of the tent into the soft tundra plants just outside. In meeting the bear, I had met part of myself. Perhaps Peter had met part of himself. Who was I, really? A creature even I did not fully know, needing to learn about myself from this bear? And who was he whose arms held me? Now a different person after our experience? We lay there together, still under a spell, until in the same way as it must happen for each creature in this wild place, sleep overcame us.

Perfect Pulpo

[Mexico]

Suzanne LaFetra

"Once you have sautéed meat, it becomes second nature. It just becomes part of you." Julia Child

Even though we couldn't get The Food Channel, I learned a lot during the four years I lived in a house topped with palm fronds. I learned that boa constrictors really like sausage. I learned that ants—a river of them four feet wide—can sweep through your kitchen and leave it scoured and crumb-less. My neighbors just shrugged; of course the ants come out during the rainy season. *Sí, claro,* you should always have a machete handy in case the snakes come sniffing around for scraps. Sometimes, things got so bizarre, I felt like an extraterrestrial. And there was no way in that steamy beach town to even phone home.

Fifteen years ago, Tulum was a shy Mexican fishing village, still relatively unscathed from the throngs of tourists visiting its glitzy northern sister, Cancun, eighty miles away. The town's butcher shop was painted sea blue, and advertised its purpose with a picture of a pig wearing a poofy chef's hat and clutching a meat cleaver, trotting after a smaller, presumably more succulent relative.

I couldn't even stand to buy stuff there for my dogs, the stench in the tropical heat was so intense.

So I learned to do my grocery shopping in the ocean. Usually I could persuade a sturdy boatman to sell his bounty to me, pre-cleaned, scaled, skinned, and filleted, paying a little extra to avoid the icky task of transforming a flopping silver creature into something I could sizzle up in a frying pan. But occasionally, my fisherman neighbor, Diablo, would offer to share his catch with me, complete with eyes, guts, bones, and tail. I often had little idea of what to do with these presents, but I was really stumped when he pulled a *pulpo* (octopus) purple and slimy from the depths of a dripping burlap sack.

"*Para ti,*" he grinned. It looked like something from another planet.

"Oh, thanks," I said, trying to look grateful. Diablo could have sold it in town for a pretty peso to someone who actually wanted it. To refuse his gift would have been insulting, and it just wouldn't be neighborly—*mi pulpo es su pulpo*.

His wife, Ceci, yanked a second pulpo from the bag, and eyed it eagerly, turning it over in her hands, surveying it as I might have done with a flawless cantaloupe.
"Perfecto," she declared, and planted a kiss onto Diablo's

sunburned cheek. She turned to me, "Do you like ceviche de pulpo?"

Ceci had been friendly with me from the start, but had become suddenly suspicious of my culinary tastes one afternoon when I had impulsively thrust a bunch of freshly harvested basil under her nose. "Isn't it wonderful?" I gushed. I was thrilled with my little crop, and it was impossible to buy in the area.

She wriggled up her face in horror. "Ay," she turned away, "but that's only for the cemetery." I didn't invite her over for a caprese sandwich.

Ceviche is a zippy, refreshing version of our boring ketchupy shrimp cocktail, but in Mexico, you make it with all kinds of sea creatures, pulpo being a favorite. I did love ceviche, but I hadn't even considered the menu, so mesmerized was I, watching Diablo expertly do some rather brutal looking things to the two octopi he had caught. Actually, ceviche sounded perfect; cool and simple, precisely the opposite of what I was feeling.

"I'll de-brain it for you, Susi," Diablo said casually.

"Gracias," I said in a very small voice. One more dexterous twist of his knife, and I saw a golf ball-sized gray mass plop to the jungle floor. The next thing I knew, he was passing me my pulpo. I reluctantly reached out with both hands, wondering just how to hold on to the slippery gift.

"No, asi," he said, "hold it here." He had two fingers hooked underneath a flap of skin (the head?) so it wouldn't slither away. I crooked my fingers too, and a moment later was transporting an octopus across the yard.

Alone in the kitchen, I laid the jelly-like thing in the sink. It didn't even look like an octopus. It was long and limp and a translucent pale pink, like a wet ballerina costume. It definitely did not look like the neat little purple rectangle that I had eaten at sushi bars. Where to begin? Even *The Joy of Cooking*, which chronicles how to slaughter a goose, couldn't help me out with this eight-legged wave-dweller.

I picked it up again, using my front two fingers "à la Diablo," and while inspecting it, I noticed something. Something awful. In spite of the fact that my neighbor had kindly done me the favor of ripping the poor thing's brain out (thus leaving the handy finger hold), the creature still seemed to be *alive*. I watched with horror as some sort of fluid pulsated under the skin. Disgusted, I flung it back into the sink, and was just about to race to the beach and hurl the monster back into the sea when Ceci chirped over the wall, "Oye, Suzanne, make sure you pound it real good, so it won't get tough when you boil it." Ah, a clue. Pounding. Boiling. I now had a starting place.

First, I thought, I should rinse off the goo. I held it under the cold water, and tried to push the slime down its body, like working the shampoo out of a long braid. After a minute or two in the rinse cycle the creature still seemed to be producing slime. I kept squeezing, wringing, and rinsing, but there was no noticeable difference. So, I gave up and resigned myself to a slippery meal. Since I didn't know what else to do, I decided it was time to move on to the "boil" part, remembering of course to "pound it real good" first.

I glanced around my sparse kitchen. On the dish rack were two pots, one big knife, and a rusty cheese grater. I didn't have a garlic press, let alone an octopus pounder. I considered my toolbox—a hammer? This seemed just a teensy bit too much like second-degree murder, so instead I opted for that ubiquitous Mexican tool, the Coke bottle. Several weeks past, I had watched, delighted, as a resourceful beach colleague adeptly mashed potatoes with one.

I gripped the bottle firmly by the neck, whacked dinner once, and immediately was showered with goo. Slime flew everywhere. I prayed for a pre-wrapped spinach and feta salad to drop from the sky.

But my ego was determined not to let common sense prevail, so I continued savagely "tenderizing" my octopus. If there had been any non-rusted metal in my kitchen, I might have seen my reflection, a psycho bringing my weapon down again and again, spattering and staining the walls with each thwack.

I considered asking my neighbors exactly how they managed to create a desirable meal out of such a mess, but then of course I'd have to admit that a) I was an inept foreigner who definitely did not belong in their beachy paradise, and b) like so many Conquistadors before me, I had taken their gracious offering and turned it into something grotesque.

Finally, slimy, disgusted, and decidedly un-hungry, I plunked my pulpo into a simmering pot of water. I peered in and half expected the thing to crawl, B-movie like, tentacle-over-tentacle out of the pot. I clapped a lid over the opening, and cranked up the heat. At last, I had tamed the beast. And I needed a beer.

I pulled a chair up near the stove, sipped a cold Bohemia, and watched the pot. Eventually the part of my brain that controls the higher, less animal, functions was jump-started, and I began to prepare the other ingredients for the octopus ceviche. I sliced white onions, squeezed limes, and pulled delicate cilantro leaves from their stems. Handling this vegan portion of the meal made me feel calmer, but I began to sweat when I noticed a purplish foam bubble up from under the pot lid.

How can you tell when an octopus is "done"—wiggle the drumstick? I lifted off the top, and looked inside. What was now in the scummy water bore no resemblance to the creature I had started with—this pulpo was a hard, curled, knob, half its original size, and reddish purple, just like the rubber chew toy my dogs used to squeak off with. I speared it with a fork and lifted it, dripping, onto my cutting board, where it would suffer the final indignity in its transformation into my supper.

Wielding my weapon, I paused—Do you cut off the tentacles? And what about those alien little suction cups? How should you handle the head? I settled on chopping the whole thing into half inch pieces, except for the beak (*beak*!?) which I quickly brushed into the garbage. Then I scooped the whole mess into my waiting bowl of onions, et al. A stir, more salt, another squirt of lime, and then at last I gratefully pushed the whole thing out of sight into the dark of the refrigerator.

The dirty deed done, I surveyed the scene of the crime. Then I scrubbed my hands, the sink, and even the walls, Lady Macbeth-like, in an attempt to remove all traces of my murderous cooking. After I had cleaned up both the kitchen and myself, I cracked open a second beer, and felt better.

I strolled out to the backyard, admired my pelt of fresh soft grass successfully taking root over the rocks. I smiled at my prolific vegetable garden, teeming with sunburst squash, eggplants, tomatoes, and of course the slandered basil. I felt less out of place, seeing the ways I had in fact bent the savage jungle to fit my civilized desires for pesto and veggie quiche.

But I knew I wouldn't be able to enjoy the ceviche. The very thought of eating it was enough to send me scampering to the *farmacia* for Pepto Bismol.

The birds in the tulipan tree started up their evening clatter, the jungle equivalent of the quittin' time bell. Federico showed up, strode through the kitchen, and opened the fridge, reaching in for a Coke. He rolled the icy bottle along his sweaty forehead and paused in the cool of the box, surveying its contents. "Oh hey," he said hungrily, "Pulpo ceviche. I didn't know you could make that."

He served himself a big plateful of pulpo, while I puttered around in the garden, sprinkling water on the baby eggplants. "Come here—Amor, this is fantastico," he shouted toward the porch. I walked back inside, and he snaked one arm around my waist, scooping up the purpley chunks with fresh tortilla triangles. "Now *this* is *comida auténtica*." He heaped the praise on me higher than the ceviche topping his chip. "It's so much better than that basil pasta you made last night. You're practically a native Tulumeña now." He punctuated his enthusiasm with a friendly whack on my ex-pat buns.

I wanted to be able to celebrate my victory over the pulpo, to bask in my boyfriend's culinary compliments. But I couldn't take a single bite. I couldn't even stand to watch Federico eat it. I went back outside and climbed into the hammock, and swatted at the mosquitoes that were enjoying their carnivorous dinner. The brightest of the stars were beginning to come out, as the brief tropical sunset quickly faded to indigo. I could see Venus that evening, while I listened to my lover devour the meal I had made.

Recipe for Ceviche de Pulpo

You'll need:
1 octopus
a helpful neighbor
a sturdy enough ego to admit when you're clueless
1 Coke bottle
1 body length rain slicker and face protection
2 onions
3 tomatoes
1 bunch cilantro
2 limes
2 serrano chiles
salt

Pound and boil your de-brained octopus. Combine with the last six items and refrigerate. Serve with tortilla chips and enough beer to eradicate all memories of your cooking horrors.

Where Light Germinates
[Peru]

Melissa Heisler

Where Light Germinates: translation of Poqen Kanchay, *from the Quechua dialect*

My massage therapist often told me of the trips she took to Peru to work with a shaman. These stories caught my attention because I was running out of options for my own health and a Peruvian shaman sounded like a valid course of action—or at least as valid as taking out organs and ingesting chemicals. In a moment of desperation, I decided traveling 3,769 miles and working with a South American shaman might be my last hope.

In the month before leaving for Peru, I was instructed to consume a very strict diet. No caffeine, chocolate, alcohol, red meat, spicy foods, and many more no no's. I think I had chicken, rice, and green vegetables for dinner every night. It wasn't easy, but I did feel better following this menu. The restricted diet was mandatory so that I would be able to work with plant medicines. Like the American Indians in their use of peyote, Peruvian shamans use San Pedro and Ayahuasca cactus for energetic and spiritual journeys and cleansings. It was important to have my system ready to accept the power of the plants.

With one oversized backpack, a water filtration bottle, and a floppy hat, I headed to Peru. At the airport, I met some of the people traveling in my group. They all appeared very granola, hippy, and earthy. My corporate-America-speak seemed out of place. I boarded the plane and called my husband. He was at a local bar with some friends, and I could hear loud music and laughter in the background. We seemed worlds apart.

I flew from Miami to Lima, and then hopped a plane from Lima to Cusco. It is a cool flight. The airplane takes off and then continues to ascend. I don't think we came down to land in Cusco. We just stopped climbing. About this time, the 11,000 feet above sea level altitude started to kick in and I became a little dizzy. As our bus took us from the airport to Poqen Kanchay, my home for the next two weeks, I was stunned by the abject poverty outside my window. Families gathered by a dirty stream and appeared to be doing their laundry. I could not tell if the blankets strung up on lines were just drying or if they were also shelter for the evening. My heart broke for these people.

We came to a corner and someone said, "There it is: Poqen Kanchay." The building was made of simple, unpainted, man-made cement and covered with the thick dust of Peruvian winters. What had I gotten myself into? Would my accommodations be just a modest step above the people we had seen near the river? As we walked from the bus into the courtyard, I felt like I was Dorothy in the *Wizard of Oz*. Nothing inside was like the dingy black and white of the outside. Instead, we were in a courtyard surrounded by a lush garden filled with irises, roses, and other beautiful plants. The walls of the courtyard were gaily painted in bright earthen colors of orange, yellow, and green.

Smiling staff members greeted us and immediately rushed to take our bags and hand us a cup of warm tea. Being a control freak, I tried to carry my own bag, but that was not going to happen here. At first I thought it was Latino male courtesy, but the longer I was there, the more I experienced, maybe for the first time, being cared for completely.

After a sumptuous lunch, two local shamans conducted a *dispacho* ceremony. It was all in Quechua so I could not understand any of it. But a shaman explained that this was an offering to Pachamama to ensure success for our journey.

After a light dinner, I slept well until the next morning. Most mornings I was the first to rise so the entire garden courtyard was mine to enjoy. The ever-present *mate de coca* (coca leaf tea) was usually ready to brew, and I would enjoy a cup while journaling before breakfast.

The plan for our second day was a cleansing in the city of San Pedro. Naively I expected this to be a ritualistic ceremony like the one the day before. Nope. This time we were to participate in a communal event using *agua minero* (medicinal water). We arrived at a municipal park and paid about one U.S. dollar plus the cost of a glass and toilet paper (if you did not bring your own). Then we all filled up our cups with mineral water and drank glass after glass until we needed to defecate.

It was a cleansing all right. I don't know if it was because I was such a tight-ass control freak unwilling to let go or because of my fear of public outhouses, but I had almost twenty glasses before making my first trip to the bathroom. The bathroom had two rows of unisex stalls. Inside each stall were two metal footprints. One was supposed to stand on the footprints, drop trou' and then let 'er rip. Afterwards, one grabbed a bucket of city water to wash away any leftovers. For four hours at the location and for another four hours later that day, the power of this natural colonic did its trick.

After that experience, we went to the ancient site of Raqchi. While there, we all huddled in the remnants of a round hut. Someone began humming and the others joined in. It was a vibrationally resonate hum, not a bubbly Top Forty hit. I didn't know what was going on. I guess I should have known that there would be religious practices during this trip, but my focus was solely on finding relief through the shaman so it really hadn't crossed my mind. Anyway, the group was humming and I tried a bit, too. After a while, I could feel the vibration in my chest. At one point it felt like the sound was not coming from me but as if it had come into existence on its own. But then again, maybe that was just the altitude messing with me.

Day three brought my first experience with the San Pedro cactus. After a large breakfast, Don Theo, the owner and shaman of Poquen Kanchay, talked about how making judgments, even pleasant ones, can lead to pain. When we make judgments, we are classifying not only the item we are talking about, but all other items in that category. For instance, if we say we like blue, it automatically means we dislike the other colors. If I say you are beautiful, it infers that everyone else is ugly. With these words, Don Theo started a ceremony that included setting our intention or our goals for the day. One by one we were given a cup of bitter, barky San Pedro tea quickly followed by a larger cup of a mint tea chaser. Immediately, I felt the warm San Pedro enter my digestive system.

After that, we took an hour-long bus ride to Tipón, the Temple of Water. At Tipón, the sound of running water was exhilarating and intoxicating. The terracing and waterways were amazing. We sat for a while and listened to Don Theo speak of how two civilizations prior to the Incas had built Tipón without the cement and metal tools of the later conquering Spaniards. An expert in archeology and anthropology, Don Theo questioned how we classify the advancements of civilizations marked by their advent of pottery, yet the pre-Inca civilization created Tipón which harnessed glacial streams centuries before they ever had pottery. He continued to talk, but I missed what he said because the plant medicine had begun to take effect.

I felt queasy and lightheaded. My ears seemed plugged and open at the same time. During the ceremony I had set an intention for peace, serenity, health, and purpose. The experience of the plant gave me the feeling of peace and serenity. I was very relaxed and didn't want to speak. I felt my voice would break the quiet calm stillness which now engulfed me. As we walked, we passed by one area where the water was beneath us, poking through some beautiful stones. I was overcome by emotion. I was told by one of our handlers that my heart was expanding. While walking around, I kept repeating my mantra of peace, serenity, health, and purpose, but I was unconsciously replacing the word "health" with "love."

At the top of the first ledge at Tipón, I looked down at the three waterfalls below and thought of how much my husband would have enjoyed this place. Then a cloud of sadness descended on me as I went into a "pity party" because I was experiencing this alone. As soon as that thought entered my mind, I started crying. Then I heard my voice saying, "No. I am not alone." (At least I think it was my voice and I think it was aloud, but no one else seemed to notice so I am not sure.)

I had expected San Pedro to be like an LSD experience where plants would grow lips and talk to me. Instead, it felt like my heart was talking to me and telling me how we are all connected. I am part of each of those rushing streams. I am part of those puffy clouds. I am part of those magnificent mountains. I was not alone at that moment, and I will never be alone as long as I can remember that I am connected to nature.

Okay, so that was a bit "woo-woo, touchy-feely, granola, hug-a-tree-ish." But it happened. We can debate whether I had a truly otherworldly connection with nature or whether the plant medicine shut down my left brain releasing the feeling of right brain connectedness. You choose. I am just sharing what I experienced because it was the first time in my entire life that I felt the peace and serenity and acceptance of just being.

The restaurant we stopped at for lunch looked similar to the rough exterior of Poqen Kanchay. However, inside it was as upscale as the trendiest restaurant in the biggest U.S. city. The food and the service were exceptional. After being fooled again by outside appearances, I began to think about the people by the river the first day. Was my perception wrong? Should I have assumed that because they appeared not to have a lot of money that they should be pitied? It turns out the longer I stayed in Peru, the more I found that Peruvians are some of the happiest people in the world.

Before I left for Peru I had seen *The Simpsons Movie*, which includes Homer's shamanic adventure with an Inuit woman and the "ephipha-tree" (Homer's rudimentary understanding of an "epiphany"). With this cartoonish image in my head, I prepared for my first experience with Ayahuasca, also called the vine of death. We had a light dinner, and then I was told to bundle up because the room was cold and the plant medicine makes one colder. The ceremony starts late in the evening. Being on Ayahuasca makes one sensitive to light so it is best taken at night.

That night's ceremony was to focus on cleansing. I thought of everything I wanted to release: being a perfectionist, taking care of others before myself, being both critical and a victim, and of course, my poor health. I wanted to let go of all the hurtful, harmful, embarrassing things I had said and done in my life. Armed with a jacket, hat, and gloves I joined the others in a room that was lit by a single candle and where all the windows were blocked by heavy blankets. Taking Ayahuasca is similar to San Pedro, but the taste is a little more bitter and there is no chaser—although I laughed when they offered a Tic Tac after the tea to help take away the nasty aftertaste.

As I felt the herb enter my body, I became queasy. It felt like a major drinking binge that was about to erupt into bed-spins. Even though there was still only one candle, I could now easily see the faces of those twenty feet away from me on the other side of the room. Once the plant really kicked in, I started hallucinating. Trying to stop the images seemed to make the queasiness worse, so I tried to go with the flow. It appeared the whole room was filled with water. It wasn't a scary "I'm drowning" thing, but more like watching a really big fish tank. I watched the dolphins and stingrays float by and tried to rock with the water so I didn't get sick.

In each Ayahuasca ceremony, Don Theo and another shaman called people up one at a time to work with them individually. This first night I was called. Standing in front of the shaman, I was told to say my full name two times. He then asked me to walk backwards. I kept walking and walking until I thought I would walk out of the room. Then I heard the shaman gasp and tell me to stop. I gathered that somehow walking backward allowed the shaman to see our lives and histories. The further back one walked, the further back the trauma.

Don Theo asked if I was married and how was my marriage. "Yes" and "good," I responded. He then told me that I was holding myself back. He asked if there was a trauma or accident when I was younger. I could not remember anything. The other shaman began to work. He waved a condor feather all around my body trying to remove all of the self-protection and self-restraint. My experience ended with a massage therapist moving her hands from the back of my head down my body to the floor and then having two other people spit-take Florida Water at me.

After that, Don Theo and the other shaman worked with several other individuals, and then played music for us. The first song sounded like a funeral march for my old self. The other songs made my head spin. I felt myself crying, but it was more of a silent scream. Basically it was not your normal Tuesday evening.

The next day, I tried to remember what incident had sent me hiding into myself, but I could not come up with anything. I now felt as if I had a hairball around my heart that was making my teeth and shoulders hurt, so I went back to the shaman. He told me the pain I was experiencing was from my inability to release. We discussed how I was trying to live my life in the framework society and my family had constructed. I needed to release that framework. This made sense to me because it aligned with all the work I had completed through counseling. So I was ready to "let go" mentally. But it was my heart that was holding me back. So Don Theo started work on my heart by blowing tobacco smoke and Florida Water at my chest, and by prescribing a special rose petal tea for me every morning.

The plant, tea, and insight all began to have their effect as I began to slowly chip away at the apparent failures in my life and began to redefine what success looked like to me. What was funny is that this perfectionist did not start imagining a new career, a sizeable sum of money, or some other tangible description. Instead, success began to take the form of being true to myself, having a pure heart, being grateful, finding time to be in nature, being positive, taking care of my body, being calm and peaceful, and slowing down so I was no longer a stress-monger. None of these states were natural to me.

My next experience was at the beautifully terraced Pisaq. Among the ruins of the manmade structures, there is a series of perfectly carved stones arranged in what may have been an ancient chamber. Something drew me to these stones. As I stood within this structure I began to sway. It was such a powerful and uncontrollable experience that I became frightened and ran to Don Theo. He instructed me to go to a nearby waterfall and wash myself. He told me to breathe out to release what was bad and to picture an open window around my heart.

As I drew water to my face, I felt emotion and pressure build in my chest. I used my hands to push this emotion down, not touching my body but working on a force just outside of my body. I pushed harder and harder, again and again, until I felt the pressure decrease and disappear. It was as if I were pushing layers of mud off my body. But this mud was unseen and untouchable. I began to feel liberated that day, free of my past, unafraid of my future, peaceful, and calm. Just as the first day's colonic had removed the buildup of food and toxins in my body, my experience at Pisaq removed the energy buildup so my energetic-emotional system could work perfectly again just as it was designed.

The theme for the second Ayahuasca ceremony was health. My guess is that my health depended on sleep because that is what I did during most of the ceremony. They said to try to stay awake, but I really couldn't keep my eyes open. The only memorable part of the process was a voice like the one at Tipón that said, "I am done crying for my childhood." I felt that I was now done living in the past, being a victim and keeping myself from moving forward. Don Theo mentioned that working with plant medicine is always different. When you expect a specific outcome, you miss the true experience. We were working with the power of the plant, not a specific effect. The experience differs depending on one's intention.

An important note about Peruvians: they eat a lot of eggs. Or at least they fed us a lot of eggs during our stay. One day we had eggs for breakfast, eggs in three different parts of the lunchtime meal, and a quiche for dinner. Funny thing is back in the States, eggs upset my stomach. But halfway through my stay in Peru, I had only two bad egg incidents, and they weren't that bad especially taking into consideration that we ate eggs constantly. This was the second time I was consciously aware of how my body reacts not just to food, but to the emotions and thoughts I have. As my mental pain eased, so did my physical pain.

One of the last sites we visited in Peru was Q'espiwara. This is an old initiation site and not a usual tour stop—not that much of what we did or saw was on the normal Globus Tour. *Q'espi* means mirror or reflection. *Wara* is the name of the initiation clothing worn. The site was beautiful. It was at the bottom of a valley guarded by tall ancient trees. I marveled at the now small and insignificant stream that trickled in the chasm left by a powerful river which once cut out the steep jagged walls. Closer to the start of the basin there was a collection of rocks which were surely the remnants of a waterfall. Across from the rocks was a huge stone with an intricate carving. I am still amazed at how the stones were carved so precisely without the use of metal tools.

As I sat on a large rock overlooking the carving, Don Theo said to let the waters wash away our pain. I closed my eyes and slowly my head lowered. Then my body began to rock and spin. The water of the ancient river was used to ritualistically cleanse our minds and spirits. When I rose from that rock, I felt at least ten years younger! There was no muscle pain or sloped shoulders from aging. The stomach ailments I'd come to Peru with were gone. My footsteps were easy and seemingly effortless. My mind was clear. My energy was high. I think I could have flown back up the mountain if I'd tried! I was recharged that day. I had finally shed the anger, fear, doubt, pain, anxiety, and disappointment I had been carrying with me for years.

When we flew back from Lima and landed in Miami, I was worried I would miss my transfer so I hurried to catch my flight home. That is when I began to feel twinges of pain again. The stress of making my flights, going through customs, and re-entering the land of Starbucks and deadlines made my stomach flip. Then it hit me. I am the one creating my pain. I am the one causing my life to be less than desirable. And most importantly, I am the one who can make a change.

The Jigg's Up
[Newfoundland]

Carol McAdoo Rehme

Salmon, lobster, caribou, rabbit, and moose were served up in recipes handed down generation to generation, every savory bite a unique blend of French, Aboriginal, Scottish, and Irish ancestry.

We'd read menus all the way up the western coastline of Newfoundland, wrapping our tongues around unfamiliar words and our mouths around unfamiliar tastes: Colcannon. Brewis. Toutons with partridgeberry jam. Some dishes—fried cod tongues, flipper pie, skinned turr—my husband preferred to leave to the imagination. If he didn't recognize it, he wouldn't taste it.

Not me. A more adventurous eater, I relished the opportunity to try new taste treats. It was all part of experiencing a culture I found fascinating. So many things were different than our own.

Like vegetable gardens planted in ditches along the highway, rich black soil—fragrant and moist—teeming with root vegetables and hearty cabbage heads. Like patient cords of winter firewood stacked and waiting at the forest's edge.

"Don't you worry about someone stealing?" I'd asked a local.

"Oh, dey'd nere tek sumpkin not dere own," he replied.

The language itself was intriguing. Who wouldn't lift a brow at place names like Pick Eyes, Dildo, and Blow Me Down? In some small ports, it was a job to wade through the dialect, deciphering enough words to piece together a patchwork conversation. The flavors of the Channel Islands, Ireland, France, and Iceland seasoned their tongues. Entranced, I kept a journal of "Newfinese" expressions and colorful phrases we heard. So when the host of our bed and breakfast suggested we "pop over" to the community building that evening for a "scoff," I lifted my pen from the tablet I'd been jotting in.

"A scoff?"

"A Jiggs Dinner. The church is hosting a Thanksgiving. You'll be a bit late, but no matter. I can point the way," she offered.

With not even a hint of trepidation, I accepted the invitation, excited to participate in a traditional Newfoundland Thanksgiving.

"What a great opportunity," I whispered to my husband.

"If they serve cod tongues, I'm out of there," he replied.

We were greeted at the entrance where we paid our fee. "Money fer de church," the elderly man explained as he ushered us through the door.

Long tables lined the crowded hall, but chattering folks waved us toward two empty seats and encouraged us to fill our plates. I didn't need to be prodded. The most heavenly aroma had greeted us outside and I could hardly wait to dig in. We joined the line at the serving tables where we heaped our plates from bowls and platters.

A Jiggs Dinner, someone explained, was a traditional Sunday and holiday meal, a one-pot meal of salt beef and winter vegetables. Cabbage, potatoes, carrots, onions, rutabaga, beets, and turnips.

"Oh, you mean stew," I said.

"Not stew. It's biled dinner."

"Okay. But what's this?" My husband poked a hesitant fork at the curious pile of yellow on his plate. He nudged a dense slab of dark bread. "And this?"

"Pease pudding is t'one. Tothern's my mudder's figgy duff."

We learned that the split peas as well as the dark molasses bread had been boiled in pudding bags right along with the meat and vegetables, absorbing and flavoring each other.

"Remarkable," we both agreed as we savored each fragrant bite.

But other aspects of the evening were more familiar—a real taste of home. A politician worked his way through the room, fawning over babies. We listened and grinned when he repeated the same joke at each table. Men swapped stories while women traded recipes. Ladies brought out a spread of calorie-laden desserts—cookies, pies, and cakes. Although I didn't recognize exotic ingredients like bakeapple and cloudberry, the cooks affected the same balance of modesty and pride I'd witnessed during church potlucks in our home town.

"Maybe I'll get another sliver of this crowberry pie," I said to no one in particular and started to push back my chair.

"Stay where ya're tat. Oi'll bring ya some."

I looked into the sparkling eyes of the gray-haired woman at my left and nodded my agreement.

And I glanced around the room at all the smiling faces. So many nice people we'd met, traipsing through the Maritimes. Food, language, scenery—so many differences separated us. But, in my quest to notice, point out, and log those differences, I'd given short shrift to the cultural similarities: openness, kindness, friendliness. An eager willingness to help.

I grinned at the woman's offer as she headed to the dessert buffet. "Thank you. And…make it a generous slice, will you? I've grown to love the food here."

A Trembling Voice

[Costa Rica]

Frank Izaguirre

Only less than a decade ago, as many as a dozen leatherbacks lumbered ashore each night of the nesting season. They came when the moon was highest, reliable as the ebb and flow of the tide. But they were nearly all gone. Even in the past ten days, the peak weeks of the nesting season, there had only been three.

The park's official name is Parque Nacional Marino Las Baulas de Guanacaste. Las Baulas means leatherback turtles, and Guanacaste is the name of the dry northwestern province of Costa Rica. The sickle-shaped beach is known locally as Playa Grande, the leatherback turtle's prime nesting site along the entire Pacific coast of the Americas.

The leatherback is the most ancient of the seven species of sea turtles, belonging to a different family than the other six. Its name comes from its leathery carapace, which allows it to travel quickly while surfing ocean currents. Its lifespan is unknown, but some scientists believe it approximates our own. The leatherback is a critically endangered species worldwide. The Pacific population is on the brink of extinction.

I came to Playa Grande with Rosa, whom I had met shortly after returning from my first time living in Costa Rica. Rosa is a New Yorker, from the city. She always looks well-dressed in her carefully selected boots and blouses. She walks more comfortably in high-heels than in flip-flops. But Rosa never balked when I told her about my fascination with the rainforest and Costa Rican nature. She listened attentively. I think it was part of her attraction for me. She was intrigued.

Two years after I'd returned from my semester in Costa Rica, Rosa had chosen to spend a semester there herself. Rosa studied Spanish language literature, so every opportunity to be in a Spanish-speaking country benefitted her résumé. I'd come to visit her, and when her classes finished she let me choose where to go. I convinced her to volunteer with me, but I don't think she'd agreed because the work appealed to her. She felt obliged.

Volunteering at a national park was something I wanted to do, but a big part of my decision to go with Rosa was because I hoped the experience would stir in her that same sense of wonder that was a part of me. She liked my stories about the places I'd visited, my interest in other living things. I felt confident she already shared the enthusiasm, that it was merely hiding beneath the surface, and if we went together to some fascinating place she'd find it. I thought Playa Grande and its charismatic leatherbacks might be the right place.

But that had not been the case, and I couldn't blame her. We patrolled the beaches at night, when the turtles lay. The few times we'd been allowed to go out, we were told to tag alongside staff members. I felt like a dog being taken out for a walk.

Most of the time we took care of secretarial duties in the office, organizing tours to observe the few turtles that were still arriving. We'd met just a few of the staff, including Rotney, the park director. Once, during the hours we spent waiting by the office, I flipped through the pages of a huge hardcover book about the world's sea turtles. There was a picture of Rotney in his Costa Rican park ranger uniform, with a caption describing his work at Playa Grande. We were in an important place, but what we were doing was not.

In an effort to generate enough revenue to hire a large enough team to regularly patrol the beach against *hueveros* (egg poachers), the Costa Rica national park service (SINAC) guides nightly tours during the nesting season to observe the leatherbacks laying. Costa Rica has an impressive national park system, and allocates a much larger proportion of its national budget to environmental conservation than other countries in the isthmus, funds freed up from the abolishment of their armed forces. Nonetheless, SINAC is a perpetually cash-strapped organization, and it showed in their equipment and facilities.

The cabin where they'd housed us was almost comically decrepit. The toilet had no seat. The mattress was more like a giant sponge than an actual bed. My favorite coffee mug had a broken handle. One night, a raccoon crawled in through a gaping hole in the roof and found a midnight snack in the kitchen.

None of that really bothered me. Actually, I thought it was endearing. Rosa didn't seem to mind it much either. She laughed at the missing toilet seat, and even at the raccoon after we'd charged into the kitchen wielding flashlights and my pocketknife. But she was tired of night walks where we did nothing besides follow someone else around. On one of our last nights, while shuffling behind a ranger, Rosa's voice nearly blended in with the gentle sway of ocean waves.

"Frank," she whispered, hesitantly, "I think we should go."

I felt frustrated, almost betrayed, but not by Rosa. I'd wanted the experience to expose her to the wonders of the natural world. I wanted her to understand my excitement for living things, and maybe share it, too. But if anything it seemed only to be solidifying the opposite feeling.

I didn't respond, just listened to the ocean's rhythmic melody, clinging to a fading hope the waves would bring in the fascination and excitement I had hoped for. We walked further up the beach, and just before it was time to turn around and return back down the beach, radio chatter broke the night stillness. A leatherback had been spotted. We hurried to the site not far from where we were, stumbling through the shifting sand in the dark.

When we arrived, I noticed just a few dim silhouettes at first. As I slowed down and came closer, I saw there was a crowd arranged in a wide circle. Many asked the rangers if they could take pictures, even though they'd been told beforehand that the flash would cause the turtle to abort her egg-laying. They kept murmuring to each other, sharing their excitement at seeing a living thing so close to its own end.

I wanted to protest, but I knew fifty people paying twenty-five dollars each is a handful for a park badly in need of new equipment. So it became little more than a spectacle, the final efforts of an ancient species struggling to leave enough progeny to last one more generation, a tragedy on display. I wondered if even more tourists would come the rarer the turtles became. Would they pay an even higher fee the closer they were to extinction? How much would someone pay to watch the last leatherback nest?

Rosa didn't attempt to break through the crowd and look. Despite my own feelings, I angled in. Seeing a leatherback was still impressive, an enormous black profile on the beach, like a dinosaur had lumbered out of the sea. A spray of sand hit my face, launched by the turtle's strong forelimbs digging its nest amid the crowd. It felt shameful to watch. I thought volunteering would feel righteous, work of both consequence and beauty. I thought it would leave us feeling enriched.

We walked away from the crowd into the darkness. The waves lapped gently beside us. "I'm looking forward to leaving," Rosa said softly. I felt sorry, and guilty.

I wanted to leave, too.

On our last night, Rotney surprised us. He said we'd be going with him to patrol a different beach, Playa En Nombre de Jesús. The park staff had swelled with the return of some of his more experienced volunteers, making it possible to patrol a beach they normally weren't able to, and because of the moon's cycle, he knew black turtles would be laying. He warned us it was a beach with *hueveros*.

We piled in the truck, excited by the unexpected new experience. The vehicle veered off onto an even muddier road through rainforest. While driving, Rotney told us this was a beach that no one knew about except his staff, the *hueveros*, and the turtles. They were trying to get it accepted as a reserve by the government, but even if they succeeded the poachers wouldn't be deterred from taking eggs. It always came down to him needing more staff.

When we arrived, Rotney sent Rosa and the other volunteers north along the beach to count how many turtles were laying or had already laid in that direction. Rotney took me to do the same down the longer southern stretch.

The arrival of a turtle can be spotted by the wide tracks it leaves in the sand. If there's a parallel set of tracks, then it has returned to the sea. The tracks can identify the species just like any land mammal, mostly by differentiating between the size of the print left by the flippers and the spacing between each track.

All the tracks we saw belonged to black turtles, which are a Pacific subspecies of the green turtle, although some experts claim they're a separate species. The green turtle is named after the color of its fat, highly regarded in French cuisine. There were no enormous leatherbacks there because the inlet to the beach was too narrow for them. They prefer to lay on wider beaches.

As Rotney and I counted, the only sounds were the steady rhythm of the waves and the pressing down of our boots through the moist sand. With the outline of the forest that signified the end of the beach in sight, we came upon a set of tracks flanked by another set of prints. Footprints.

We reached the nest. The mess of dug up sand confirmed it had already been sacked. Despite the number of times Rotney had said there were *hueveros*, it hadn't seemed believable. The idea of poachers seemed to belong to a more distant world. It couldn't occur there, where I was. I looked to the forest, wondering if he watched us from some hiding spot we could never find. Maybe he'd been dodging Rotney and his crews for years, and would for years to come.

Would he feed the eggs to his family? There were many poor people in this area, despite the luxury hotels on Playa Tamarindo just a few miles away. Or would he take them as an aphrodisiac, thinking them a cure for impotence? Sometimes they're sold to tourists on the black market as a "cultural experience." Maybe he just liked the way they taste. Turtle egg shots are popular in parts of the country.

Excluding the one before us, we had counted eight nests already laid and three still in the process. Rotney told me to follow him back up the beach to the truck to get some equipment. He asked if I didn't mind getting my hands a little dirty. "Claro que no," I said, intrigued, and followed him back to one of the previous nests we had visited.

I lay prone, the right side of my face pressed against the mound of sand before me. My gloved hand reached into the hole I had dug into the nest until my arm was in a little past the elbow. My palm faced upwards and waited for the pair of eggs to drop. There they were. They always came in pairs. I felt them for a moment. They were rounder than chicken eggs, more spherical, less pointed. They were soft and slimy, covered in fluid from the turtle's birth canal. It was definitely the most intimate I'd ever been with another species.

I carefully removed the eggs and placed them in the large plastic bag at my side. I had already collected four or five dozen. Rotney told me to expect about seventy eggs total, so the turtle was close to finishing. I had to be very quiet and still so as not to disturb her, or she'd abort and return to the sea. She knew I was there, but as long as I was calm she would keep laying. And she did.

I could see Rotney standing to my left a few meters away, watching, though I couldn't see the expression on his face through the darkness. We had headlamps with red bulbs that didn't bother the turtles, but they were kept off to conserve batteries unless we absolutely needed them.

When nesting, turtles are disturbed by conventional white lights. All sea turtles avoid beaches with light pollution from hotels and condominiums, which might now be more common than beaches without them. Even in Costa Rica, with its sterling environmental reputation, there were many beaches that had been developed within the past couple decades and no longer supported turtle nesting, like the nearby Playa Tamarindo, which had historically been a huge nesting beach for leatherback, black, and olive ridley turtles. Though the town has boomed with a steady flow of tourists, no more turtles go there.

Most of the seven species of sea turtles nest in complete darkness to prevent predators from eating both them and their eggs. The waves eventually wash away their tracks and conceal the location of the nest.

Another pair of eggs fell into my waiting hand, and I wondered if on another part of the beach slimy eggs were slipping into Rosa's hand, too. She wouldn't like it, just as she hadn't liked the entire trip.

A strong flick of sand against my cheek notified me she'd finished laying and was covering her nest. It was empty, but the eggs would be safe where we were taking them. I withdrew my arm and slowly stood up. The other volunteers had dug a hole that would be invisible to the *hueveros*, who were able to see where the turtles nested but not the carefully concealed holes the volunteers had made, where we reburied the eggs.

The turtle finished covering up her nest, wheeled around, and faced the shoreline. Her solemn duty accomplished, she began her dignified march back to the sea. The waves lapped at her as she approached, calling her back. I could make out less of her profile with each new gush of spray that swept over her body. As she inched forward, the waves began covering her entirely. I could see her for only a moment when the water receded, until finally I didn't see her at all. The ocean had claimed her again.

I wondered if she'd return from thousands of miles away precisely to the point I still stood on to lay again next year. Or maybe she'd be caught in an industrial fishing net and strangled, or suffocate on a plastic grocery bag she mistook for a jellyfish. Maybe she'd be harvested for her fat. Whatever her fate, I was glad to have been there with her then.

Rotney's hand on my shoulder startled me. He spoke softly, suggesting we go see how Rosa was doing with her second nest of the evening. I couldn't respond. I couldn't imagine they had forced Rosa to remove the eggs from even one nest. She had asked to remove the eggs from a second?

I followed Rotney's profile up the beach, trudging through the sand until I made out the silhouettes of a few other volunteers beside a turtle. Rosa lay flat on the sand behind the turtle just as I had, hand extended into a hole dug beneath the turtle's body. I knelt down next to her, and saw her bright smile flash in the dark. She whispered in a trembling voice I'd never before heard, "I brought life into the world."

Horse, Horse, Tiger, Tiger

[China]

Ferida Wolff

One summer, my family went to China. None of us spoke Mandarin, the official Chinese language. At our request, our Shanghai guide taught us how to say "Hello," "Goodbye," and "Thank you." The Chinese people like to bargain, she said, so she also taught us to say, "How much is that?" and "That's too expensive." We learned the Chinese equivalent of so-so, which would make it seem as if we were not too eager to buy and we would not be cheated. What she didn't teach us, and perhaps couldn't, was how to listen with Chinese ears.

In America, we accept many different pronunciations and still understand what is meant. It is the word itself that conveys its meaning. In China, it is the tone of the character that makes the word, and depending upon which tone is used, the meaning changes. The character *ma*, for instance, can mean you are calling your mother, asking a question, naming a horse, or saying something offensive.

So armed with our new linguistic knowledge, we headed off on our own into the shops that lined Nanjing Road, a major shopping area in Shanghai. In one shop, we pointed to a fan. The clerk took it from its case to show to us. We looked it over and carefully said in our best Mandarin, "Mao, mao, hoo, hoo." The clerk's eyes widened. She backed away into the protection of the other clerks who were standing around stone-faced trying to decipher our intentions.

Afraid that we were creating an international incident, we quickly bought the fan and forgot the bargaining. We tried our language skills in another store. This time the clerk burst into laughter and repeated our statement loud enough for everyone around the counter to hear. They all laughed. We still didn't get it.

We were laughed out of a few more stores in a few more cities before we stopped trying to bargain. We couldn't figure out what was wrong. We'd said what our guide had taught us, hadn't we?

We finally asked another guide in the resort city of Hanghzou why we were getting such reactions. When he heard what we said, he laughed, too.

"What you are saying is, 'Horse, horse, tiger, tiger.'"

He pronounced the words slowly for us to hear the right way to say them. We listened very carefully this time and said the phrase exactly as he taught us.

"No, no. That is not right," he said.

We tried again with equally disastrous results. We couldn't hear the difference. A dip in intonation (if we heard it at all) was, for us, just another way of speaking. But for our guide, it was a whole new word. He shook his head and gave up.

We stopped verbally bargaining for the rest of the trip, but found that through gesture and intention, we were able to purchase what we wanted. And finally we were rewarded with smiles instead of laughs.

Open Eye
[New Mexico]

Lynn Pinkerton

Some persistent murmur deep in the ordinariness of our days yearns for a break in the monotony of our lives. Feeling trapped by the rhythm and routine of clocks and calendars, we want to go where ships go when they slip out of sight.

Stalked by my own mundane voices, I set out several years ago to find plump, juicy adventure in the high desert promise of northern New Mexico. My spirit was feeling worn down by the sameness of my days. The same skyline, same voices, foods, music, dreams, schedule. I was hopeful that red canyon sanctuaries and Native American ghosts would infuse my sometimes dreary world with fresh, sparkling splendor and new found perspective.

For a week, I devoured enchiladas laced with roasted ancho chilies, embraced the sanctity of adobe missions, pondered ancient petroglyphs, reveled in the infinite, unbridled blue sky, warmed beside piñon-scented fires, rode the rhythm of a drumming circle, and was filled with certainty that this enchanted place held the beauty and magic missing from my daily life.

On the final day of my trip, I booked the last available space to tour the home of legendary artist Georgia O'Keeffe. Tucked away just off the dusty, unpaved plaza in the tiny village of Abiquiu, the approach to O'Keeffe's home rambles through a jumble of broken-down trailers, dilapidated cars, worn-out homes, a faded library, an old adobe church, and three scrawny, forlorn-looking dogs. Perched on an unassuming mesa, the original home was built in the eighteenth century, later expanded, and then restored by O'Keeffe when she bought it in 1945. Surrounded by still-lush gardens, the sprawling adobe home is sparse and reflects O'Keeffe's minimalist approach to her life and her painting. At first glance, nothing indicates that this simple, unadorned dwelling gave birth to many of the iconic artist's best-known and most loved paintings.

However, as I followed our tour guide from one sparse room to another, I began to see things differently. O'Keeffe's flinty, enduring spirit seemed to lead the way through her studio, bedroom, living room, kitchen, and courtyard. Aided by large, stunning reproductions of O'Keeffe's paintings, our guide repeatedly held up a new one and then pointed nearby to the original inspiration for the painting. All well-known images. The *Patio With Black Door*; Pedernal, the flat-topped mesa that O'Keeffe called her private mountain; cottonwood trees along the Chama River; The White Place; a sun-bleached cow skull; the road to Santa Fe. She found magnificence and splendor in the simplicity of the ordinary that presented itself every day. A flower, a rock, a mountain, a desert-seared bone, or a bit of sky.

Inspiration and joy offered itself just outside her window. On the patio. A stone's throw from the backdoor. I found myself intrigued and inspired by the idea that she instinctively knew that the search for truth and beauty does not require a full tank of gas or a passport. It only requires a willing presence and an open eye.

In the Footsteps of Fossey
[Rwanda]

Irene Morse

We crest a small rise and there he is: across a clearing in the rain forest and above us about twenty feet, he sits upright, presenting his beautiful silver back. Everything about him exclaims strength. His muscles ripple beneath a luxurious fur coat. His massive head turns upward slightly, perhaps to catch the mid-morning sun on his face, perhaps to show his imperious nature. He is magnificent—and he knows it. His name is Guhonda, and he is the largest Silverback Mountain Gorilla in the world.

My husband, Gary, and I have traveled twenty-five hours on three airplanes, covered more than 10,000 miles, spent twenty-three frigid hours in Brussels, crossed the width of the African nation of Rwanda in a Land Rover, and climbed nearly 1,000 feet up the face of Sabinyo Volcano through foot-deep mud for just this moment.

As my breathing returns to normal, I begin to describe to Gary, who is blind, the amazing creature that is so studiously ignoring us. Were Guhonda to stand upright, he'd be roughly five-and-a-half feet tall. He weighs in at just under 500 solid, muscle-bound pounds. His long, dark fur shades into silver just beneath his shoulder-blades, turns to salt and pepper on his rump, and then is black again. Mountain gorillas develop their silver backs at maturity, about age twelve, when they are ready to mate. Until then, they are called Blackbacks.

Guhonda's face, ears, hands, feet, and chest are smooth and shine like polished leather. His nose looks flattened, pushed in by some unseen giant hand. Guhonda can be specifically identified by the wrinkles, lines, and nostrils of his nose, which create his "nose print." It is as unique to him as fingerprints are to humans. He is the patriarch and protector of the Sabinyo Family of mountain gorillas.

It has taken us two hours to hike (or as they say in Rwanda, trek) to this spot on the mountain. Each of the seven gorilla family groups in the Parc National des Volcans can be visited once a day by a maximum of eight people. However, we are supported by a crowd of assistants. Two heavily-armed soldiers travel with us to watch for "unfriendly" poachers. Each of us has a porter to carry our backpacks, water, camera equipment, and extra layers of clothing and rain slickers. We have two park guides. One, the aptly-named Patience, is Gary's personal guide in case he needs additional assistance.

Gary and Patience set the pace through gently sloping farmland. Although we gain elevation, the thirty minute hike through fields of potatoes and other row crops hardly prepares us for the mountain. We scale a sturdy rock fence that delineates the park boundary, and the terrain immediately changes. We are at approximately 3,000 meters (9,800 feet) of elevation. Within a few yards, we enter a thick rainforest and locate a narrow, muddy trail. Up the mountain we lumber, wading in sludge, avoiding buffalo "poo," and gasping for air, another 275 meters (900 feet) or so.

We stagger into a tiny clearing where our porters are waiting for us along with the trackers who have been following our Sabinyo Family since before dawn. Communicating with our guides by walkie-talkie, they have directed us to this place and indicated that the gorillas were just up the mountain a few meters. We stand a moment to catch our breath in the thin air before surrendering our walking sticks—the gorillas might mistake them for weapons—and make our way to this area where Guhonda and his family are enjoying their bamboo brunch.

Gary notices the group before they come into sight. They have, he reports, a pungent, although not unpleasant, odor and we hear occasional soft, throaty sounds. These mountain gorillas employ about twenty-five vocalizations. Our guides have learned these vocalizations and are able to communicate with them in a rather rudimentary way.

Behind and slightly above Guhonda, are Gukunda and her baby, Isheja Big Ben. Because these gorillas are Rwanda's greatest natural treasure, many resources are given to their protection and much ceremony attaches to the naming of the babies. The traditional naming ceremony, Kwita Izina, is performed each year for those infants born during the year, and celebrities or notable political figures are often given the honor of choosing a name. Isheja Big Ben was named by a British dignitary last year.

Gukunda reclines easily and munches on a piece of peeled bamboo while Isheja Big Ben climbs on her, pulls at her fur, and generally behaves like a lively toddler.

Off to the right, Gihishamwotsi, a young Blackback, is cavorting in the lush vegetation. We've been told that he's nearing maturity and is very energetic and mischievous. I've seen the film *Gorillas in the Mist*, and I've read *No One Loved Gorillas More*, an account of Dian Fossey's work here. I've been told that these animals share ninety-eight percent of their genes with humans, but I am not prepared for how playful they are, nor how gentle.

While we stand—mouths agape and cameras clicking—watching these giants go about their daily activities, our guides are quietly "speaking" to them. They make a guttural sound in their throats, almost a growl, which means, to a mountain gorilla, something along the lines of, "We come in peace and mean you no harm."

Quietly, Patience moves to stand in front of me and extends his arm and hand in front of Gary. At that moment, Gihishamwotsi comes sprinting down the trail in front of us, running upright. I barely have time for a gulp of air before he disappears behind a bend in the trail, but I'm pretty sure I hear him "tee hee-ing" as he goes. Later, he circles around and comes down the hill behind part of our group. Using the element of surprise to his best advantage, he shoves against Amy, grabbing a handful of buttons from her shirt as he streaks by.

We are allowed only one hour with the gorillas. The government of Rwanda and the guides, trackers, and porters stress the care and well-being of the animals. Dian Fossey and other naturalists and veterinarians have lived with, protected, and studied these mountain gorillas since the late 1950s. Although the gorillas have become habituated, our visit is limited so as to not stress them.

So all too soon, we reluctantly retrace our slippery footsteps down the mountain. Patience is enjoying the adventure of trying to keep a blind man on his feet as they encounter mud, poo and feet-entangling vines on the steep trail. Laughing, they invent a game called "Slip, Slide, Step," and amazingly, Patience is successful most of the time.

Rwanda means Land of a Thousand Hills and our eco-hotel, Virunga Lodge, is perched atop one. From the lounge, made cozy by the warmth from a giant fireplace, we enjoy a spectacular view of the Virunga volcanoes and the mist-filled valleys made famous in the book and film. Far below us, the scenery surrounding us is reflected in the stillness of Lakes Ruhondo and Bulera.

The next morning, we arrive at park headquarters early to visit the gorillas again. This time we are greeted by a small cyclone of activity. The word is out that, for the first time ever, a blind man has come to trek the mountain gorillas. There is great excitement over the event.

Gary and I are ushered into a tiny office and introduced to Bonny Mukombozi, a young journalist with Rwanda's daily English-language newspaper, *The New Times*. Although his English is fairly good, it is difficult for him to understand why a blind man would want to visit the gorillas.

When the interview is over, pictures must be taken: Gary with me; Gary with Ged, the owner of our tour group; Gary and the Park Warden; Gary and Eugene, the Deputy of Tourism, and others. Eugene will be Gary's official guide today, but Patience, who is, after all, experienced in all this, will come along as back-up.

After another two-hour climb, we come to a small clearing and there they are. This is the Hirwa, a fairly newly formed family consisting of a Silverback, five females and five babies. The exquisite (as yet un-named) Silverback sits just opposite a female who is facing us. He is grooming their baby. This is unusual. We are told that Silverbacks rarely groom the babies, but this one is engrossed in the task.

He grasps the baby's two ankles in one enormous hand (just as humans do when changing a diaper), upends the youngster, and lightly grooms his backside. He picks at the baby's fur, and then gently—oh, so gently—strokes the baby's tangled, unruly hair into place.

After a few minutes, the baby wriggles free and runs to the female, climbing on her, beating his little fists against her chest, and resting his head on her shoulder. He cavorts between the two, entreating them to play with him.

Ged and Patience slip softly through the bamboo to the opposite side of the clearing. Ged is taking pictures of our group with the gorillas in the foreground when there is an imperceptible change in the behavior of the Silverback. Patience puts his arm out slightly in front of Ged and whispers, "He's going to charge."

Suddenly the Silverback rises up to his full height and dashes directly at the two men. He covers the ground in an instant and, just before colliding with them, stops as suddenly as he started. He looks directly at them for an instant, and then turns and saunters into the foliage. We learn that this is not unusual behavior; the gorillas will charge if people get a little too close—to challenge one another, or just to be playful. They rarely make physical contact even with each other. Still, it takes a minute for my heart-rate to return to normal.

A tiny guy hitches a ride on his mother's back, his legs splayed nearly horizontally across her massive frame. A youngster lies on his back, one foot in the air, examining his toes. He pulls his foot toward his face, loses his balance, and then rolls down a soft embankment. Mothers and babies alike stand and slap their chests for the sheer joy of it.

Suddenly Kabatwa, a female, moves toward us. Patience speaks softly: "Just back slowly down the trail. She only wants to pass." We've taken one or two cautious steps backwards, when we hear rustling behind us. Another female and her baby have moved into a small stand of bamboo and undergrowth a few feet down from us. Taking stock of our options, we notice that there are gorillas to the right and left of us as well. We are completely surrounded by mountain gorillas.

We stand perfectly still. Kabatwa is sitting upright about three feet in front of us, and I look into her face, trying to get a sense of her. Her eyes, like those of all the gorillas, are bright, shiny orange with flecks and swirls of brown. There is a tiny black pupil in the center. They remind me of marbles, aggies, I played with as a child. Her lips are thin, arranged in a permanent smile and her distinctive nose dominates her face.

We stand quietly, examining one another, until our pathway down the trail is clear. Kabatwa rises to her full height, a few inches shy of five feet, and pushes past us.

We have been allotted an extra twelve minutes because of this encounter—twelve precious minutes for an amazing experience. It is difficult to describe all of the emotions one can experience at such moments. Suffice it to say that it was a singular life experience that I will never forgot: I stood next to a 300 pound gorilla and was not afraid. But for now, it is time to make our way back down the mountain.

There are only about 750 mountain gorillas left in the world and they are all located in the Virunga volcanic mountains of Rwanda and the Democratic Republic of Congo (the border runs through the mountains) and in Bwindi Impenetrable Forest in Uganda. The gorillas are considered extremely endangered.

Driving Compassionately

[Bali]

Peter Marmorek

Bali is sometimes known as "the land of smiles"—and it is true, people here do smile at you a lot. Then they yell "Hello!" while you walk, cycle, or drive past them. And if you say "Hello!" back to them, they smile even more.

At first I wondered if young children were taught in school to yell "Hello!" at foreigners. This isn't quite as far-fetched as it might seem. They teach "tourism" as a subject in school in Bali, and a good way to start any subject is by giving kids a sense of their power and how they can use what you've taught them. You start by teaching them "Hello!" and gradually work your way up to, "Would you like to sign up for the diving special to the island coral reef today?"

But the Balinese not only smiled too consistently for it to have been an affect taught in school, they also smiled at one another, and the older adults smiled and said, "Hello," to tourists as well, albeit without the violent enthusiasm of the children. So this friendliness to the other seemed to be an authentic Balinese trait.

Once I'd figured that out, the driving patterns started to make a lot more sense than they had previously, when they'd seemed like a thousand chaotic accidents just waiting to happen. But they never did, which left me glad but puzzled. The chaotic part was the disregard for lanes. The standard Balinese road is two lanes wide, with the houses (and children, dogs, chickens) all no more than two meters away. There are about three times as many motorcycles as four-wheeled vehicles on the road, and they are all passing one another (as well as pedestrians and cyclists) more or less continually.

The basic guideline is to stay as far to the left as you can. But you can't help feeling uneasy when your driver is in the wrong lane passing two motorcyclists (one of whom is passing the other) while a car is coming head-on towards you, passing a motorcyclist in its lane. That's the chaotic part. Then the oncoming car slows down enough so your car can finish passing and pull over in front of the motorcyclist who has also slowed down to let you get in front of it. It has a certain element of the grace of Balinese dancing, and it consistently works, which is the amazing part.

In North America, we are taught to drive legally and to follow the rules of the road, such as "stay in your own lane." If you go out of your lane to pass, you get back as fast as you can. If someone is overtaking and is driving towards me in my lane, I honk and flash lights to alert him that he's in the wrong place and that he needs to get back into his lane. I will of course slow down or drive onto the shoulder to avoid hitting the idiot, but only with a keen sense of being wronged by some bloody asshole who clearly doesn't know how to drive. And I think that's the way most of us on our continent would react.

Timothy Leary once astutely commented that if we were taught to drive lovingly, we wouldn't need all the rules that tell us how to drive legally. At the time I thought it was just an amusing conceit, but in Bali that seems to be how it's done. The goal is for everyone to arrive as fast and safely as possible, so drivers are watching and working with the pattern of vehicles on the road, rather than just focusing on their own car. There is a lot more honking here, but the honks don't mean "Look out!" or "Stop what you're doing!" as they do at home. Here they might better translate as "I'm here," or perhaps even "Hello!" The assumption is that if everyone knows where everyone else is, we'll all work together to make the highway work.

In North America, we drive as individuals separate and distinct from the other individuals with whom we share the road. But in Bali that awareness of the other that starts with three-year-olds yelling "Hello!" at strangers, has evolved into a way of driving communally with compassion. And it works a lot better than rule-based driving does, which is very interesting indeed.

Pickles and Hiccups

[On the way home]

Randy Richardson

"Pickles," chirps the two-year-old strapped into the car seat behind me.

eye him from the rearview. He can't be hungry. He just munched down a pack of fruit snacks.

Moments later, "Hiccups," he utters. I glance at my wife in the passenger seat next to me. She cranes her head to see what is going on in the back seat. "You have the hiccups?"

In the rearview, I see him crack a smile. "Pickles and hiccups." He giggles uncontrollably. Did we let him bake in the sun too long? We are on our way to the airport to go home from Florida after our first family vacation.

"Pickles and hiccups," he repeats, triggering another round of giggles.

"What's so funny?" I ask.

"Pickles and hiccups," he replies, as if the answer is obvious.

His giggling is contagious and spreads to the front seat. The long car ride must be getting to all of us. This is how it has been all week, like when our son discovered the simple joy of putting ice cubes down his shirt. These are the moments I take home with me and store away forever. Not gift store trinkets or the shells we collected off the beach.

Family vacations are not like the vacations I went on before I became a parent. They are, in some ways, not vacations at all. Certainly not the idyllic vacations pictured on the covers of those glossy travel magazines I drool over at the newsstand. There is little rest and even less relaxation, but there is lots of play. You find yourself in the pool instead of sunning in a lounge chair beside the pool. Instead of kicking back with a tropical drink, you smile in wonder at the sight of your little one kicking his little legs in the water as he learns to swim.

The joy of a family vacation is that you get to act like a kid again. The pain of a family vacation comes when the realization hits that you no longer are a kid.

We have a late flight home and we are all tired after the two-hour drive to the airport, two hours at a nature conservancy on the way, and three hours at the airport. When the boarding call sounds, we are all ready to go home. Except our son, who is, apparently, ready to go, but not home. When he stands in that distinctive squat, that parental alarm goes off in my head. My wife's wary eyes simultaneously catch my own, and then our son makes the official call: "Pooh-pooh."

Stay calm, I tell myself. The plane won't be taking off for twenty minutes. There's no cause for concern.

Wrong. Mommy is frantically searching through the backpack.

"I don't think we have another diaper," she says.

"How could you not pack enough diapers?" Sometimes in a panic, words come out that you wish you could recall. This is one of those times. "We've got to do something and do it fast. The plane is boarding." Sometimes that button inside our brain that stops us from saying dumb things gets stuck. This is one of those times. My wife shoots an annoyed glance. "We could just wipe off the poop and reuse the diaper," I sputter, struggling to find the functional brain that used to be in my head.

My wife gives me a look of incredulity. "We can't just wipe off the poop and reuse the diaper," she calmly explains. Then, as if she's stepped into a phone booth and changed into a superhero uniform, she takes control. She locates nearby parents. Surely they must have extra diapers. No. She grimaces, and then scans the vicinity for little munchkins. There are none to be found.

"We've got to do something," I say, throwing in my final, worthless, two cents.

My wife nods, certain now that she's married to the Dumbest Man on the Planet. The clock is ticking. She sees no other choice but to scoop up our child and to scamper to the restroom.

Meanwhile, I'm sitting there literally holding all the bags, nervously looking at my watch. The airline attendant calls the last boarding group number. We're going to miss our flight, I'm certain of it.

An iconic Hertz rental car commercial from the mid-1970s featured O.J. Simpson, long before his criminal trial for murder and other legal troubles. In the spot, Simpson runs through an airport, leaping over rows of departure lounge seats, in an effort to make his plane. That is the image that comes to my mind when I spot my wife off in the distance, carrying our two-year-old boy, who is flapping his arms and laughing like a hyena. To a toddler, frantically racing through an airport terminal is, apparently, even more fun than saying pickles and hiccups.

"Did we miss the flight?" my wife asks, breathlessly.

"No," I smile, "we can board now."

The airline attendant had minutes earlier called our boarding group, the last one. As we made our way onto the plane, my wife replayed her heroics for me. On the way to the bathroom, she spotted a family with a toddler. She stopped, desperation dripping from her eyes, and asked if they had an extra diaper. They did, and it was even the right size.

Family vacations, I realize now, are not about the destination. They are about how you get there and back, and the precious moments in between. They are about spending time together, as a family, and laughing about pickles and hiccups.

Treks

[Kathmandu]

Katherine Horrigan

It is our first day in Kathmandu. We walk the dusty streets in the midst of brown and red chickens and the heart-breaking dogs of the Third World. Our destination is Bahktapur, an ancient walled city.

A shirtless old woman massages oil on her legs, toothlessly chattering to the old man sitting by her side. A goat sits in a second story window, surveying us below. An old man makes his way across a roof top garden, like a character in a Philip Glass opera. Daily animal sacrifices take place in front of an elaborate shrine. Blood stains on the ground provide proof. Afterward, the believers hold a barbecue.

After a week on the trail, our head sherpa becomes ill. Three porters take turns carrying him down the mountain to his village, passing him from back to back in one of the wicker-like baskets used to haul our tents, food, and cooking equipment. He is brought home in time to see his wife, his baby, his parents. After one and a half hours, he dies.

He must have been sick before the trek, they say. If so, are we in danger of dying from the same disease? We hold a ceremony in a darkened tent, a group of strangers trying to mourn together, uneasy now, our eyes avoiding contact. For this moment of spiritual congress, we seem more apart than together. A few days later we contribute money for a ceremony. We sit against the wall in a monastery, drinking yak butter tea while monks pray and chant, their long loud horns discordant.

The next day I follow closely behind Tenzing, the second in command. When he stops and crouches on the ground, I watch him bend a twig into a semicircle and coax a tiny bug onto the twig. I hear the other trekkers behind us, grumbling, asking why the holdup. Tenzing puts the bug-bearing twig on a rock at shoulder height, and watches the bug crawl away, now safe from certain death from a trekker's boot. He gives me a great big smile before he turns back to the trail, the signal for us to join him in this our processional as we move up, up into the Himalayas.

Back home, I take my clothes to the dry cleaners. When I open my car door, I notice a ladybug making its way across the vast dusty expanse of the parking area. I find an envelope in my glove compartment and after a little jostling, the ladybug comes aboard, its black and red vivid against the white. I walk carefully to a small patch of grass at the foot of a guy wire, bend down and release my catch into new life. I watch the bug creep forward in the grass for a minute before I get back into my car.

Virtual Travel
[On the Internet]

Trendle Ellwood

Gladys and I took a class outside during field biology. She shared with me an interest in everything that grows, so we smelled the wild root beer aroma of three-leaved sassafras, tasted dandelion flowers, and touched green moss. We identified poison ivy and stinging nettle, and then squished the juice out of their counteragent, jewelweed.

One day as Gladys and I were talking, I mentioned that I have hardly been anywhere except Southeastern Ohio, Missouri, and back again.

She grinned and said, "But girl, you sure did find a lot to love right where you are." I guess she is right. The diversity of the wild things that thrive in our little corner of the world amazes me. I told her I have no desire to travel because I detest highways. So Gladys will be surprised when I tell her that I have become a world traveler.

It all began when my youngest looked up our address on the computer via Google map and did something that I didn't realize you could do. She pulled the figure of a man to the street and suddenly we were looking at our home in 3-D just as if we were driving by in a car. It was eerie as we went past our yard and looked right at our front door. I can tell that the photographer came by last summer, because that is when I had sunflowers growing by the barn. You can turn and scan my view of Farmer Scholl's field, look down at the road or up at the sun in the arc of the sky. You can even see our honey sign.

You can take a ride such as this anywhere in the world that Google has filmed. I have not been to Missouri for twenty some years, so I moved the little symbol of a man to the map and rambled the road that drives past the place where we used to live. The appearance of your destination will depend on the day the photographer passed through. They caught my Missouri on an overcast day, the trees leafless and bare. In this scene I journeyed past the old home place and found it not only smaller then I remembered, like places from our past so often are, but also empty. I tried to find the lane I lived down as a young bride but I got lost. I clicked out and took my journey to sunnier skies.

Mountains touch the sky in Norway where in my cyber journeys I stay off the highways and travel rural roads. I love visiting places where the architecture is different. In Mexico you can see thatched roofs, in Italy tiled, and there are roofs covered with plants in Switzerland.

I also learned that the garbage can did not evolve the same everywhere in the world. Some places have triangular garbage cans and others little square boxes.

I am very interested in plants, so every place I go I zoom in to see if I can identify the specimens alongside the roads. I wonder if Hawaii has a dry season, as it was not as lush as I imagined. There is a tree that grows there that stands like a sentinel on the hills. I wish that I could get a good zoom in on its leaves because I would like to know if it is in the cedar family.

Google should bring along a botanist to label the plants in its outings. It must be Golden Marguerite blooming on the steep mountainsides of a lovely road, which I cannot even believe is a road, it is so narrow, in Italy. I am certain that the trail up a mountain (I am partial to summit views) on the island of Las Palmas de Gran Canaria is lined with the same intense blue lobelia that I buy at Smeltzer's greenhouse every spring. Amazing to know that there is a place where it grows free and in abundance.

As much as I cherish nature, I start feeling a little bored on my cyber journeys if I have gone a few miles without seeing any signs of my own kind. When I see a homestead up ahead my attention is awakened. One day I cybered through a village on the Indian Ocean in a place with flora and fauna very different from what I know. And there on a staircase overlooking the water sat a woman with graying hair, a little boy on her lap. I didn't have to wonder for one moment what family they were from. On the other side of the world a little boy brings springtime to a woman in her autumn, just like my grandson does to me. Their skin and eyes are a darker color, and I am sure they speak a different language, but are we so different? It seems obvious that our grandmother hearts know the same sorrows and the same joys.

So I have to tell Gladys that I have traveled a good deal of the world now, and I see that there are many places on this beautiful earth that God made that I could love. There are places where strange and exotic plants grow, but what I find the most interesting is that everywhere in this whole wide world there are people much like us.

Nowhere

[Drifting in the heavens]

William Hillyard

"¿Cuál via?" he asked, "Which way?"

The question was a little unsettling. Not so much because I had no idea where we were, or, for that matter, where it was exactly we were going. Nor, really, because we were floating in an eight-foot aluminum dinghy in the flooded jungles of the upper Amazon, in the remote, third-world blackness of night. It was because the guy who had only a moment ago asked me if I had a flashlight and had, at least until they ran out, been illuminating our way with paper matches, and finally, in the frustrating darkness asked me "Which way," was my guide. The guy who was supposed to know which way. The guy, you know, I paid to get me here.

Where was "here"? My estimations put us some 100 miles upriver from the Peruvian town of Iquitos, then a dozen or so miles up a small tributary and then perhaps a few hundred yards off to the left.

Why was I there? Well, that's another question entirely. I recall being asked that question once before, in the foothills of the Himalayas in Burma. Well, he wasn't asking me, exactly, why I was there. Rather, he was asking me, I guess, as spokesperson for all us nomadic wanderers, why we go there…why we travel. He simply could not understand why we came there, of all places, to his little isolated corner of nowhere. The people there lived simply, got up at dawn, cooked and farmed, went to bed at dark. Why ever would anyone want to come there to watch them? That question jolted me with an electric shock. Why do we leave our comfortable homes just to see some far-away stranger's home? What compels us travelers to go through the significant expense and discomfort to go someplace simply because we've never been? British climber George Mallory in 1924 answered this question rather flippantly: "Because it's there," he'd said. That's not an answer. Everest didn't accept it either and Mallory up there remains.

Well, why was I here? Instead of bobbing around in that banged-up boat in the flooded jungle, I should have been by then at a small rainforest camp located on an oxbow lake somewhere off a remote Amazon tributary—this tributary, here, I figured, where we were lost. I had spent what to my guide must have been a lifetime's fortune to get here.

I'd made arrangements with him after asking around the docks of Iquitos. He knew the camp I wanted, he'd said, and agreed to take me. He never asked why I wanted to go there, nor could I have answered. Oh, I could have said something about the rare pink river dolphins said to inhabit the area, or the Yahua Indians who lived near there, but he didn't seem to care. In silence, I loaded into that guy's tin-can dinghy and at 4:30 in the afternoon left Iquitos. I never learned his name. We skipped over the orange water at thirty miles an hour, the late afternoon sun coloring it and the trees on the shoreline and the cottony clouds. The wind at that speed was delicious. I estimated about a three hour trip, meaning we'd arrive sometime after dark.

Here, some 2,000 miles from its mouth at the Atlantic, the Amazon spreads for more than a mile, tree-line-to-tree-line. Its flow is surprisingly swift, and in it whole trees and great rafts of flotsam—masses of vegetation disgorged from the Andean highlands—drift by, themselves microcosms alive with fish and fowl, and peopled too sometimes, by those who ride those rafts and take their living from that exotic forage. Following the rainy season, the Andean deluge funnels into the Amazon basin and raises the water level so virtually no dry land remains. It inundates thousands upon thousands of square miles, leaving the tree canopy as islands in this vast, heavily wooded lake—the only mode of travel here by boat.

Being here, why is it so different from being at home? Well, this is the Amazon, of course. It, like our Yosemite and Grand Canyon, ranks right at the top of any list of the world's most spectacular sights. When asked why I was there that time in Burma, I hadn't the grandeur of a Yosemite as an excuse. We talked walking through golden hills, the smell of the dry grass damp in the morning air. It was beautiful, sure, but in no way unique. There was no sense of place separating it from, say, the rolling hills outside of my hometown on a summer day. We could have been anywhere, in fact. I told myself I came to visit the Shan, an area hill tribe. Because they were there?

I'd trek half way around the world to spend a few awkward hours sitting uninvited in a Shan home but wouldn't drive the few miles up the freeway to Little Saigon, only thirty minutes from my house. Arguably, the Vietnamese-Americans of Little Saigon are a unique hybrid culture found only in Westminster and its environs. But to speak of my neighbors in this way, as exotic peoples worth "going to see," smacks of racism; not so when applied to the Shan, half a world away. This stretch of the Amazon above Iquitos is immense to be sure, but quite frankly, is it really anything more than a broad plain of water flowing through a canyon of trees? This could have been any rural stretch of the Mississippi, or any wide tree-lined river for that matter. Ah, but here lived the Yahua Indians and the rare pink dolphins.

The sun sets quickly in the Amazon and it gets dark—a Biblical, primordial sort of dark. Speeding up the river, we floated in a void, the jagged, black outline of trees separated like a torn page from the lights in the firmament of the heavens above. I felt upside down, like I was hanging off the planet. The stars pulled you into them, swaddled you.

The ancient Inca found their constellations not in the stars themselves but in the empty space between them, so dense with stars is this southern hemisphere sky. These spaces, for them, formed the creatures of myth. And then there's the Southern Cross. Its appearance confirmed I was far from home. I've seen a lot of places, some thirty countries on five continents. I've crossed oceans in sailboats, been deep in the outback of Australia, but nowhere had I ever felt as remote as this, as otherworldy. Intergalactic distances we crossed, my guide and I, the cosmic wind against our faces.

My guide pointed us into the inky void of the shoreline, branches and trunks gaining form as we entered them. Idling slowly amongst the black columns of wading trees, invisible brambles whipped and brushed our faces. Our route, it seemed, took us through this jungle to get to our destination. Around and around and through the forest we bumped, match after match held aloft—my guide, the Buddha-bellied statue of liberty. The matches lasted till we were thoroughly lost.

To save gas, he killed the motor. Its silence sucked the air from the place. Deep in the flooded jungle, maybe a hundred or two hundred yards or more even from that little tributary river that was itself ten or more miles upriver from the Amazon proper, we were in a darkness without form more than 100 miles from where I should have taken the advice of the half dozen or so other boatmen and waited until morning to begin this journey. No flashlight and now no matches. Only fireflies blinked, their lights reflected in the water gave the sense we drifted, disembodied, in the heavens.

"Which way?" he asked me. He asked me, after all, because I was the reason we were there.

There was another Westerner, a woman, in Burma that time. She wore a pot top on her head. The Shan use conical bamboo covers on the water cisterns in their houses. This woman must have mistaken it for one of those Vietnamese hats, you know, the conical kind. But it wasn't. It was a pot top, and everyone she encountered, everyone who saw her, knew it. I sat floating in the firefly stars and thought of that woman. Everyone but her knew. She walked around that village oblivious. The Shan villagers stared at her bewildered.

To my guide, I guess, I was just a crazy gringo with a pot top on my head. I felt his bewildered gaze as we sat in nowhere's inky darkness, waiting in silence for the dawn.

Why was I there? I chose this over my comfortable bed in my comfortable house. Honestly, I would have chosen to come even if I had known this would happen. I'm just a modern-day George Mallory with a pot top on his head stuck in a boat in the upper reaches of the Amazon River. This was what I had come for. Because it was there.

About the Contributors

Ben Bellizzi's work has appeared in several publications, including *Canyon Voices, Monday Night,* and *Prick of the Spindle,* and was included in the "2010 Notable Reading" portion of the *2011 Best American Non-required Reading,* edited by Dave Eggers. He is a graduate of the California College of the Arts MFA program and lives primarily in northern California (bbellizzi@hotmail.com).

Jennifer Choban hails from the Pacific Northwest and graduated from Linfield College. She has worked as an early childhood educator, ESL teacher, and grant writer. Currently she lives in Guanajuato, Mexico, where she writes, hikes, engages in home-improvement projects, and attempts to improve her Spanish. You can find stories of her travels at www.gearupandplay.com.

Dominick Domingo is an Art Center graduate and veteran Animation Artist (*The Lion King, Pocahontas, Hunchback, Tarzan, Fantasia*). He's illustrated books for young readers for all the major publishers. Dominick's original screenplay credits as a filmmaker led to a growing writing resume. To capitalize on it, Dominick recently penned a collection of narrative nonfiction essays titled *Jesus Shoes*, one of which won the Solas Award for Best Travel Writing in the humor category. *The Nameless Prince*, from Twilight Times Books, represents Dominick's foray into Young Adult Urban Fantasy. He'd be happy to retire as a full-time author. He lives in the Silver Lake neighborhood of L.A., surrounded by hipsters.

Terri Elders, LCSW, lives near Colville, Washington, with two protective dogs and three narcissistic cats. Her articles and stories have appeared in dozens of periodicals and anthologies. She lived overseas for a decade in four developing countries, including Belize, Guatemala, Dominican Republic, and Seychelles. In 2006 she received the UCLA Alumni Association Community Service Award for her work with the U.S. Peace Corps. She blogs at atouchoftarragon.blogspot.com.

Trendle Ellwood travels the world on her laptop at her home in southeastern Ohio where she writes a column titled "From These Hills" for the local *Towne Crier*. She has been published in various periodicals including *Bee Culture*, *GreenPrints*, *Cottage Magazine*, *Grand Magazine*, and *Guideposts*, as well as online at www.homestead.org. On her blog at www.trendleellwood.com, she archives her country impressions. Her photography profile can be found online at www.redbubble.com/people/trendleellwood and on her website at www.ohiohomestead.com.

Kelly Hayes-Raitt was press credentialed by the Jordanian government as she entered Iraq in July 2003, three months after the U.S.-led invasion. She reported live from Baghdad, Fallouja, and Basra via satellite phone to National Public Radio, KNBC-TV, and other news outlets. Her essays about Iraqi refugees appear in several anthologies including Random House's *Female Nomad & Friends* (June 2010) and *Best Women's Travel Writing 2011*. "Still Alive" is from her forthcoming journalistic memoir *Living Large in Limbo: How I Found Myself Among the World's Forgotten.* An award-winning author, she lectures at colleges and other venues, lives in Los Angeles and Ajijic, Mexico, and blogs at www.LivingLargeInLimbo.org.

Melissa Heisler, of It's My Life, Inc., helps employees and business owners find joy, balance, empowerment, and success in their work and home lives. For employees, she educates and instills work-life balance, career exploration, and job transition. For business owners, she assists in start-up, growth, and day-to-day survival using fifteen years of product and brand marketing experience. Melissa is a monthly contributor to Women's Ally, a support community for professional women and a contributing author in *Defining Moments*. Melissa speaks to large and small groups and has appeared on local television. She offers a free inspirational e-newsletter at www.itsmylifeinc.com.

An avid traveler, **William Hillyard** has visited more than forty countries on five continents. He has crossed the equator by plane, by boat, by bus, and on foot, has battled 40-foot seas in a 35-foot sailboat, been chased by a wild orangutan in a Sumatran jungle, and stared into the black pupil of a rebel Kalashnikov in the rainforest of Guatemala. His writing can be read in the *Denver Voice*, *Earth Island Journal*, the *Orange Coast Review*, and the literary journal *Lowestoft Chronicle*. He is currently working on a book, *Wonder Valley*, set in a remote community in the Mojave Desert. To find out more, visit www.williamhillyard.com.

After receiving her PhD in 1997, **Katherine Horrigan** taught as an adjunct English Professor for the University of Houston. Both print and online journals including *The Birmingham Arts Journal*, *The Rusty Nail*, *Devilfish Review*, and *The Prose Poem Project* have published her poetry, plays, and short stories. Her poetry has also been published in the 2013 Texas Poetry Calendar, and she recently completed *Drought*, a novel set in south Texas. Kathy lives with her husband Joe in Houston, Texas, and may be contacted at mkkh@aol.com.

Frank Izaguirre is a writer, conservationist, and birder. He teaches Journalism and Creative Nonfiction at Pittsburgh School for the Creative and Performing Arts (CAPA). His work has appeared in *ISLE*, *Terrain*, and a forthcoming issue of *Fourth Genre* will feature an essay on the status of the travel writing genre. While birding around his home in Pittsburgh last week, he briefly encountered a Tennessee warbler before it flew onward to distant tropical forests in Central America. He tweets @FrankMIzaguirre.

Kathe Kokolias is a writer and an artist. She has read her essays on National Public Radio and has been published online, in newspapers, magazines, and anthologies including Travelers' Tales, *A Woman's World Again.* She has published two books: *Spandex & Black Boots, essays from an abundant life,* and *What Time do the Crocodiles Come Out.* Kathe belongs to the International Women's Writing Guild, the Hudson Valley Writers Guild, the Art Center of the Capital Region, and is co-owner of the Broadway Art Center in Albany, NY. You can contact her at kathekokolias@aol.com. Please visit her website at www.kathekokolias.com.

When the name **Dina Kucera** is mentioned, which is often, the word "genius" is regularly tossed around. When that happens, Dina will modestly say, "That's a strong word!" Then she smiles and drinks her Caramel Soy Machiato triple espresso no whip. She has been a writer her entire life and has been a stand-up comic for more than twenty years. I'm sure you've heard of her. Please also read her book, *Everything I Never Wanted to Be.*

Suzanne LaFetra is an award-winning writer whose work has appeared in numerous magazines, newspapers, and literary journals, including *The Christian Science Monitor*, *The San Francisco Chronicle*, *Brevity*, and *Rosebud.* Her essays have been included in more than a dozen anthologies. She lives in northern California with her family, and they never, ever have octopus for dinner.

A freelance writer, **Jennifer Lang** has been published in *Parenting, Yoga Journal,* and *Natural Solutions* magazines, among others. Her essays have appeared in the *South Loop*

Review, San Francisco Chronicle and *Drash,* as well as on ducts.org. Her essay "At Gilda's" appeared in the Dream of Things first anthology called *Saying Goodbye: to the people, places and things in our lives.* More recently, two of her stories were chosen for *Chicken Soup for the Soul.* Jennifer blogs weekly about making the most of her move to Israel with her family at www.opentoisrael.com.

Peter Marmorek is the author of the recently published memoir, *The Year of Living Doggedly*, the story of a man, a dog, and the year in which the one tried to train the other. He also runs *The Writers' Croft*, which offers online courses in a supportive writing circle. He lives in Toronto, Canada, with his wife, Diana, and their labradoodle, Rui. You can follow his adventures, contact him, or read excerpts from his book at http://doggedly.ca.

Irene Morse is a freelance writer who enjoys traveling in search of adventure and examining the human condition through drama and theatre. Her community theater column appears regularly in the local newspaper. She and her husband, Gary, have a large blended family. You can read about their family Christmas traditions in *Chicken Soup for the Soul, Christmas Magic.* Irene writes a monthly cooking column for an online magazine and is hard at work on a book about very different trips that she and Gary, who is blind, have taken together. Email her at irene@ingramct.com.

Lynn Pinkerton is a freelance writer who knew in the fifth grade she wanted to be a writer when she grew up. Sidetracked by careers in social services and special events marketing, Lynn eventually reclaimed her childhood aspiration, joined a writing group, and began publishing. Her work has appeared in a variety of print and online publications including *The Christian Science Monitor*, *New Southerner*, and *The Shine Journal*, as well as several anthologies including *Nurturing Paws, The Path*, and *Littlest Blessings*. She divides her time between New Chapel Hill and Houston, Texas. Contact Lynn at SLPinkerton@gmail.com.

Shannon Huffman Polson is the author of *North of Hope* (March 2013, Zondervan), a memoir of adventure, grief, and music. Her creative nonfiction has been published in a number of literary magazines and periodicals on topics ranging from the natural world to faith, family, women's issues, and the military. Polson and her family live in Seattle and spend several weeks a year at a small cabin in interior Alaska. You can find her at www.aborderlife.com.

Julie Rand lived in Japan for ten years and while there traveled extensively throughout Asia and Europe. She is an editor, organic gardener, grad student, baker of pies, and maker of soup, as well as mother to thirteen-year-old twins. She sometimes wishes she were elsewhere.

Carol McAdoo Rehme likes a winding side road where she's always alert to inspiring vistas, adventurous culinary delights, and unexpected friendships. A veteran ghostwriter, author, and editor, Carol writes from her window-banked office nestled along the Front Range of the Colorado Rockies. Her most recent projects are *Finding the Pearl: Unstoppable passion, unbridled success* and *Fundamentally Female*. Contact her at carol@rehme.com.

Randy Richardson is president of the non-profit Chicago Writers Association. His essays have been published in the anthologies *Chicken Soup for the Father and Son Soul*, *Humor for a Boomer's Heart*, *The Big Book of Christmas Joy*, and *Cubbie Blues: 100 Years of Waiting Till Next Year*, as well as in numerous print and online journals and magazines. He is the author of two novels, *Lost in the Ivy* and *Cheeseland*. An attorney, he lives with his wife and son near Chicago. For more information, visit www.randyrichardson.net.

Roz Warren's work appears in *The New York Times* and *The Funny Times*. She has also published in *The Utne Reader, The Christian Science Monitor, Seventeen Magazine* and *Beatniks from Space*, and she has edited a dozen collections of women's humor. Visit her website at www.rosalindwarren.com.

Ferida Wolff is the author of seventeen books for children and three essay books for adults. Her work has appeared in *The New York Times*, *The Christian Science Monitor*, *Moment Magazine*, and *Woman's World*, among other periodicals, and she is a frequent contributor to the Chicken Soup for the Soul series. She also writes a nature blog, which can be read at http://feridasbackyard.blogspot.com. A former elementary school teacher and yoga instructor, she now teaches stretching, has a weekly meditation group, and loves to travel. Her website is www.feridawolff.com. She can be reached at feridawolff@msn.com.

Reading Group Guide

1. What were your expectations before you opened the book to read the essays? What were your reactions when you finished the last one?

2. What does the title *Being There Now* mean to you? How does the title relate to this collection of stories?

3. What was your reaction to the collection as a whole? Did you have a favorite story, or one that you disliked? Why?

4. Which story moved you the most? Why?

5. If you have traveled, what was your most memorable trip? Why was it special to you?

6. Is there a difference between being a tourist and being a traveler? If so, how would you explain it?

7. Have you ever gotten lost while traveling? What happened? What would you have done if you were lost on the Amazon like William Hillyard?

8. Of all the places described in this anthology, is there any one place you would now like to visit?

9. Suzanne LeFetra and Carol Rehme both tried new food. One cooked octopus in Mexico and the other sampled hearty Newfoundland fare. What do eating and cooking have to do with travel? What's the most unusual food you've ever eaten or cooked while far from home?

10. Like Ben Belizzi ("A Quick and Cozy Kidnapping") and Dina Kucera ("The Happiest Place on Earth"), have you ever had anything go terribly wrong while traveling? If so, what happened? What would you have done if you were in their shoes?

11. In "Day of the Dead," Kathe Kokolias learns something about Mexican funeral customs and in the process changes the way she views death. Have you ever had an experience traveling where you changed your behavior because you experienced a new way of doing things? If so, why?

12. Both Dominick Domingo and Ferida Wolff struggled with communicating in a foreign language. Have you ever had any funny experiences while trying to speak a foreign tongue?

13. How did Jennifer Choban and her friend react to the lack of privacy in China? How does humor help us while traveling?

14. Irene Morse went to Rwanda to see gorillas; Frank Izaguire observed turtles laying their eggs on a Costa Rican beach; and Shannon Huffman Polson encountered a grizzly bear in Alaska. How were these people changed by their encounters with these animals? What did each of them learn?

15. Have you ever made friends with a person in another country like Kelly Hayes-Raitt did with the Iraqi translator?

16. Why do people travel?

About Dream of Things

Dream of Things publishes memoirs, anthologies of creative nonfiction, and other books that fulfill our mission to publish distinctive voices and meaningful books. For more information, visit dreamofthings.com.

OTHER BOOKS FROM DREAM OF THINGS

Leaving the Hall Light On
A Mother's Memoir of Living with Her Son's Bipolar Disorder and Surviving His Suicide by Madeline Sharples
"A moving read of tragedy, trying to prevent it, and coping with life after." Midwest Book Review

Everything I Never Wanted to Be
A memoir of alcoholism and addiction, faith and family, hope and humor by Dina Kucera
"Raw and funny." Joel Stein, Time Magazine columnist

"Like a maelstrom." ForeWord Review
"Malcolm in the Middle meets Cops." The Compulsive Reader

Saying Goodbye
To the people, places and things in our lives, ed. by Julie Rember and Mike O'Mary
"If you have ever had to deal with loss, read this book." Midwest Book Review

MFA in a Box
A Why to Write Book by John Rember
Winner of Hoffer, Nautilus and Midwest Book Awards as one of the best new books on creative writing
"The essential truths about excellent writing." The Judges of the Hoffer Awards

The Note
A book about the power of appreciation by Mike O'Mary
Named Best Gift Book of 2011 in the Living Now Book Awards

Wise Men and Other Stories
A collection of holiday-related stories by Mike O'Mary
Essays in the tradition of Robert Fulghum, Dave Barry, Bill Bryson and other great American humorists

COMING SOON

Daughters of Absence
Transforming a Legacy of Loss, ed. by Mindy Weisel
A collection of twelve essays written by daughters of Holocaust survivors. Introduction by Eva Fogelman, author of *Conscience & Courage: Rescuers of Jews during the Holocaust.*

Swimming With Maya
A Mother's Story by Eleanor Vincent
"Vincent's poignant decision to donate [her daughter's] organs will resonate with even hard-boiled readers, as will her movingly recounted transformation through grief and loss." Booklist

Betty's Child
A memoir by Donald Dempsey
In the tradition of *Angela's Ashes,* this memoir chronicles one child's ordeals with poverty, religion, and physical and mental abuse as he attempts to come of age with only his street smarts and unflagging sense of humor to guide him.

www.ingramcontent.com/pod-product-compliance
Lightning Source LLC
Chambersburg PA
CBHW060223180626
46813CB00007B/2935

* 9 7 8 0 9 8 8 4 3 9 0 0 9 *